ONE
BREATH
AT A
TIME

A Skeptic's Guide to Christian Meditation

J. DANA TRENT

UPPER
ROOM BOOKS®
NASHVILLE

For Joanna, who planted the seed, and for
Heather and Barbara, who watered it.

CONTENTS

ACKNOWLEDGMENTS

I always write that a book owes its life to its editor—and that remains true. This one doubles down on that mantra. While my therapist gave me meditation "homework," it was my editor, Joanna Bradley, who suggested I write about my skepticism of and struggle with this practice. Thanks, Joanna, for planting the seed. Fred and Heather, my beloved Hindu and Buddhist practitioners (respectively), continue to water that seed through modeling sustainable, diligent meditation practices for their resident Christian. Their enthusiasm for the spiritual benefits of sitting still and quietly are contagious. Barbara Jessie-Black, in guest lecturing with my Wake Tech Community College World Religions courses, also demonstrated the importance of keeping meditation accessible and simple—especially during stressful times. My brother, Ron Joines, graciously shared his medical expertise, making the body's complex physiological systems accessible to those of us without MDs. Britainy Lewman Sholl, Erin Lewman Riggs, Kate Harris, Reverend Karyl D. Estes, and Reverend Jennifer Hege served as my cheerleaders extraordinaire—phoning frequently to check in on my grief and writing as often as the Holy Spirit nudged them, which was a lot. I'm forever in debt to my Christian faith community, Binkley Baptist Church, for its eagerness to dive deeply into ancient and mystic Christianity to glean lessons for today's practice. My husband's Sri Caitanya Sanga pilgrims taught me that instead of "becoming" a meditator, I needed to just "be" one. The entire Upper Room Books family continues to be a source of support and gracious collaboration. I'm especially grateful for my authors' accountability group of Sharon Seyfarth Garner, Whitney R. Simpson, and Kristen E. Vincent. Most of all, thank you, dear reader, for giving this book and practice a try. May these words—which do not come from this writer but from a hunger to *listen* to God—feed you as much as they have fed me.

Chapter One

RELUCTANT BEGINNERS

We do not want to be beginners. But let us be convinced of the fact that we will never be anything else but beginners.

—Thomas Merton

Better is a handful with quiet than two handfuls with toil.

—Ecclesiastes 4:6

"You should try meditation."

This is familiar advice, doled out by loved ones, friends, colleagues, and, worst of all, doctors. They make meditation seem so accessible with their casual, friendly suggestion. But with my diagnosis of chronic migraine—a condition that leaves me feeling as though I have a pickax in alternating eyeballs fifteen days out of each month—the suggestion to meditate is akin to unsolicited wisdom from the well-meaning folks who might also say, "I'm not a doctor, but I play one on TV." When I show up for lunch meetings on cloudy days unable to remove my sunglasses, prescriptions unfurl. Instead of responding to my pain with, "How awful. I'm so sorry," my lunchmates propose a barrage of suggestions because they know it will be "just the thing" (be it an over-the-counter drug, essential oil, yoga pose, or supplement) to cure me forever. Moreover, they assume that this is the first time I've heard their idea.

"Why didn't I think of that?" I respond politely, even though I've already downed my allotted five migraine prescriptions and a half bottle of anti-inflammatories, doused myself in lavender oil, swallowed two tablespoons of Sriracha in lemon salt water, twisted myself into unspeakable yoga poses, and squeezed my acupressure points—all before 6:00 a.m. I understand where friends and colleagues are coming from when they offer said treatments—I'm an ENFJ who leads with Type 2 on the Enneagram, meaning I am the *helper* of all helpers. But when my therapist said, "You should try meditation," six days after my mother's unexpected death, I was enraged.

"Why didn't I think of that?" I said, instead of ripping her head off. I was hardly able to calm my mind enough to form sentences, let alone *meditate*. I'd been glued to a hospital or hospice bed nonstop for two weeks. I hadn't slept; my cortisol levels were sky-high, my body bloated, my brain speeding like a car at the Indy 500. How could I be still and breathe? I reminded myself that she meant well; everyone does.

I had been telling my therapist about my recurring medical trauma nightmares that began when my mother was admitted to a North Carolina intensive care unit for perforated diverticulitis. On that day, I had been recording an audiobook in Nashville, 500 miles from my dying mother. My editor and I wrapped up quickly; the entire publishing staff enveloped me in prayer and got me to the airport, where I begged ticket counter personnel to let me standby on the next flight going anywhere near Raleigh. Minutes before they closed the gate door, the airline obliged, sending me to Charlotte. Along the way, I awkwardly blubbered and sobbed behind sunglasses while pressed between two uncomfortable businessmen in the bulkhead, playing a loop of thirty-six years of life with my mom in my mind.

I finally arrived in Raleigh and my husband, Fred, raced me to the hospital. My doctor-brother, Ron, had already supervised more than forty-eight hours of nonstop care for Mom. As her health-care power of attorney, he advised her doctors and surgeons on her wishes, translated CT scan findings and medical jargon for me, and parsed all the possible outcomes. For the next two weeks, Ron, Fred, and I remained with Mom, anticipating her every need like she was our very own sick and fragile infant, unable to articulate her pain or go to the bathroom without us.

After my mother's death, the nightmares got worse. I'd sit up in bed at 2:00 a.m. and ask Fred, "Where's my mom?"

"She's gone," he'd say, as he pulled me close.

The dreams were my brain's carryover from the hyperalert posture of constant worry and exhaustion, where medical rooms made days and nights indistinguishable and guilt reigned. *Are we doing enough for her?* I had asked myself constantly.

My therapist assured me the nightmares would dissipate, but they were part of a normal, post-trauma response I didn't yet understand. "You need to stop the automatic thinking," she encouraged. "You should try a guided meditation practice," she added and threw out names of apps I had heard of. I resented this remedy, likening it to the migraine "cures" hurled at me in the past. But this time it was worse—because she was right.

The next morning, I began the world's most pitiful six-day meditation practice.

A Beginner's Mind

Sitting atop a gray *zafu*—a fancy meditation cushion my husband bought long before my mom died—I downloaded the meditation app everyone gushes over. I tried it—three long minutes each day for six terrible days—focusing on my breath, noticing my thoughts like cars in traffic, and withholding judgment, blah, blah, blah.

I couldn't get past the narrator's voice. He was better suited to playing a gritty Marvel Comics villain than guiding my chaotic, grief-fueled mind through a meditation practice. Had I been in a rational state, his voice might not have irritated me. Its pitch and cadence merely made him a scapegoat onto whom I could project my stubbornness and skepticism, unsure of my ability to sustain a meditation practice while drowning in grief. But I also felt annoyed by the *intrusion* of his voice—his commands belting from my iPhone's speaker, the strange cognitive dissonance of technology beckoning me to the gate of the mystical, peaceful realm for which I yearned. How could I settle my traumatized mind enough to tiptoe closer to God while the very device that buzzed incessantly during Mom's illness sat right beside me, adding to the cacophony of noise in my head? The smartphone meditation app felt like a magnetized iron rod, pulling to it every random, useless, rusty nail in my brain.

Each app session looked the same:

Breathe, Dana. Focus. Inhale; exhale. Inhale—1, 2, 3, 4.

Ignore his voice. It's not that bad. OK—it's that bad. Who hired this guy? Did he lose his job as a villain in the James Bond franchise? Did Fred and I see the last James Bond movie? Something about spectre? *What is a spectre? Queen Elizabeth's walking stick? Adele sang that theme song, right? Or was it Sam Smith?*

Breathe, Dana, breathe. Focus. Ignore his voice. Inhale—1, 2, 3, 4.

Where is this guy's pink slip? Couldn't they have cast a velvety-voiced human? James Earl Jones would have been perfect. Oh! Sally Kellerman from the M.A.S.H. movie. I forgot about her. It could have been the Jones-Kellerman meditation duo.

Breathe, Dana, breathe. Focus on the breath.

What was Kellerman's voice-over commercial in the 80s? Ketchup? No, no—it was Hidden Valley Ranch salad dressing! Poured lusciously over iceberg lettuce. Now I'm craving croutons. Can you make croutons at home? How do you get them not to turn out like the stale cubes at cheap salad bars?

Breathe, Dana, breathe. Focus on the breath. Inhale—1, 2, 3, 4. Exhale—4, 3, 2, 1.

My hamstrings are so tight. I need to do more yoga. No, ballet! Ballerinas stretch a lot. Was Patrick Swayze a classically trained ballerina? Would that have made him a ballerino? Sweet Jesus, that man could dance. "Now I've had the time of my life." Ready for the lift? Best dance scene ever.

Breathe, Dana, breathe. Focus on the breath. Inhale—1, 2, 3, 4. Exhale—4, 3, 2, 1.

Dear Lord, save me from this agony.

Agony. Aging. Agent. Agriculture. Agoraphobia. Agnus Dei—ahh that's more appropriate.

Breathe, Dana, breathe. Focus on the breath. Inhale—1, 2, 3, 4. Exhale—4, 3, 2, 1.

Agnus Dei: Lamb of God, you take away the sins of the world. Lamb of God, you take away the sins of the world. Lambs—they're so adorable and soft looking, though I've never actually touched one. But they jump on the beds in those mattress ads with such glee—or are those sheep? What's the difference?

Breathe, Dana, breathe. Focus on the breath. Inhale—1, 2, 3, 4. Exhale—4, 3, 2, 1.

Lambs! Lamb of God, you take away the sins of the world. Lamb of God, you take away the sins of the world.

Sins. Savior. Salvation. Silence. Lambs.

Silence of the Lambs! Ah—no! No, no, no! Don't go there. That was a terrible movie. I'll never get those horrifying 138 minutes of my life back. The only saving grace was that I discovered that Tom Petty song: "She was an American girl."

Breathe, Dana, breathe. Focus on the breath. Inhale—1, 2, 3, 4. Exhale—4, 3, 2, 1.

Tom Petty. Gone too soon. I hope James Earl Jones and Sally Kellerman are still kicking so they can rerecord this meditation app. They'd make billions. Hearts would melt; wars would cease. We could get this guy back to his real job on the set of The Avengers. *We'd play Tom Petty at his going away party, everyone smiling as we cut the big sheet cake with blue icing that says, "Don't come around here no more."*

Ding.

Finally, those three agonizing minutes were up, and Mr. Villain Narrator and I had accomplished nothing.

I'm not skeptical about the entirety of spiritual practices—just the ones in which I'm supposed to sit completely still with my phone beside me to calm my traumatized mind and listen for God. I can pray and journal until the end times—my brain spinning plates like an overachieving carnival worker. But I've always doubted my ability to sustain a sitting-still, ears-open meditation practice, which is different from writing and praying. How do people use these apps without launching into a silent monologue in which a very bored God is the sole audience member? How do I sit and *actually* listen, instead of hopping from topic to topic and prattling away in my mind? And, most importantly, how do I do it *every day*?

Teachers Make the Worst Students

Because I was (perhaps mistakenly) admitted to a top-tier divinity school and am married to a Hindu who's a former monastic and has kept a steady meditation practice for nearly twenty years, I've picked up a few contemplative practice bread crumbs. I've taken courses and read books on meditation and spiritual practices. I've even *taught* meditation.

As a former hospital chaplain, I learned quickly how to create, hold, and lead people through a sacred space. That skill, paired with the accumulated techniques I'd gleaned throughout the years, afforded me enough competency to *lead* meditation for groups—from millennials to senior adults. But consistently *practicing* meditation is another story.

Teaching and holding space for others to engage in spiritual practice affords me a luxury I'm addicted to: control. I'm the alert instructor, the helper—eyes open, brain engaged, proceeding from one step to the next, reading directions and leading eager meditators in and out of sessions, all while watching the timer. I'm not the one who's trying to be still or focus or be contemplative. I'm the one who's done the research, read all the books, made the lesson plan. I'm the one *in charge,* and people *need* me to be in charge. This is a teacher's true nature: We're bossy helpers who loved to be needed, which sometimes makes us lousy students.

But this teacher could no longer deny that she needed some good, old-fashioned home-work—no apps, no tricks, just *practice.* Day after day, week after week, God had sent those pesky messengers—from my therapist to the gritty-voiced app narrator—to deliver the syllabus for the class I was skeptical that I could pass: Sit-down-and-practice-meditation 101.

Prayer vs. Meditation

I love to talk. In my profession, this is a necessity; in meditation—not so much. In the classroom, I'm the professor who establishes the daily learning outcome for my students, then energetically bounces through lectures, visuals, and the lesson's application in guided discussion via the Socratic method. I ask students questions to stimulate their critical thinking; they discover and connect underlying ideas to apply them to an assessment and life. This requires a lot of emcee extroversion and speedy verbal processing. But as much as I love to talk, I needed to practice *listening*—specifically to God.

I grew up among evangelical Baptists with robust extemporaneous prayer lives, the kind where folks can (and will) talk *to* God anytime, anywhere, aloud or silently, for any length of time. I was raised to chitchat with the Divine for hours. My prayer meetings with God were then followed with journaling pages of notes, listing God's tasks. As an adolescent, I also kept a "Prayer Box"—a Belk's department store jewelry box I painted yellow and labeled with a Sharpie. It held slips of paper with the priorities I'd chosen for God—just so God was clear on what needed to be accomplished *right now.*

In as much as I was good at bossing God around, Sunday school and youth group also taught me how to "balance" my prayer life with a more well-rounded sacred "conversation" that wasn't just about requests. I learned the ACTS prayer by heart (Adoration, Confession, Thanksgiving, and Supplication), as well as the TRIP (Thanksgiving, Repent, Intercession,

Purpose) and PARTS (Praise, Ask, Repent, Thank, Share) methods. But with me still doing the talking—whether it was praise, gratitude, confession, or "Help me!"—I wasn't listening.

My prayer time was full of words and goals, not Psalm 46:10: "Be still and know that I am God!" I wasn't heeding God's "still small voice" (1 Kings 19:12, KJV). Even if I had I shut up long enough to catch a message from God, it would have had to be like 1 Kings 19:11-13, only God would need to arrive in *all the loud ways*—the shouting of a strong wind, the earthquake, and the fire—for me to notice. There is nothing wrong with a fervent prayer life, but for those of us who can't quit flapping our gums, we miss *hearing* God—whom scripture tells us arrives in the quiet stillness.

Meditation, I learned, is often *wordless prayer.* This intentional and quiet practice helps us focus our attention on God—and *listen* for God's "still small voice"—so that we may experience God's revelations. In contrast with prayer, meditation uses fewer words (or none) so that our spiritual and mental effort is concentrated on soothing the mind's chaos to *hear* what God has to say.

Practice Doesn't Make Perfect—But It Sure Does Help

My therapist was right. I needed to halt my brain and body's automatic response to my mother's sudden illness and death to begin my journey of healing. I needed to cut off my cognitive engine and pull the parking brake. But—in accordance with my control-freak, teacherly ways—I knew I had to write my *own* curriculum. No apps; no technology. I had to forge my own meditation path, one that would work for me—the restless, bossy woman who doesn't like to sit still, be quiet, and listen to God. And I certainly didn't need the added distraction of an app.

But beginnings are hard; I didn't want to start from zero—none of us does. Thomas Merton, the wise monastic and Catholic priest who dedicated his life to spiritual practice, reminds us of this truth: We will never be anything but beginners. Once I surrendered to being a meditation student—not a teacher—and, therefore, a beginner, I found something refreshing about being a novice. I could simply make *progress*—which is the job of all students—and no one (including myself) should or could expect faultlessness. I crafted a meditation plan that worked for me based on a beginner's curious mind and *wabi-sabi,* the ancient Japanese practice of imperfection. Children instinctually understand the wisdom of being a novice. Before they hit puberty and become self-conscious, they will try *anything* for the mere intrigue of it, without worrying about getting it "right." Adults need this reminder: Meditation is a *practice*—not an exercise in perfection.

After thirty-six years of deep Christian faith and fervent prayer, my most sincere effort in *listening* to the triune God was birthed from an urgent need. But I also realized it came from a place of hunger, a lifetime of yearning to go deeper. No matter the inciting incident, we must travel our own fledgling trails. Our meditation practice—just like our unique relationships with God—is unlike anyone else's. We are all beginners—and always will be.

How to Use This Book

This book provides you with the framework and structure to be a beginner. I designed a lesson plan, providing a safe learning environment for you to explore various meditation tools in a nonintimidating way. This book draws on and is inspired by scripture, Jesus' practice, ancient and modern approaches to meditation—from Eastern traditions to early Christian monastics to Christian mystics—and, finally, twentieth-century Centering Prayer. I've gleaned wisdom from all these threads and woven them into an accessible forty-day practice for folks like me, who are skeptical they can be still and listen for God.

By sharing my own reasoning (and reluctance) for trying meditation, I hope you feel encouraged to consider why you felt drawn to this book. Why do you want to embark on this journey? Does your brain feel cluttered and loud? Are you physically and mentally stuck in overdrive, living in a 24/7 culture of go, buy, do? What purpose or intention do you bring to your meditation practice? Are you hoping to listen for and discern God's voice? Take a moment and consider what is propelling your interest, curiosity, or need.

Chapters two and three make the case for meditation, differentiating it from prayer, but also providing a strong foundation on the role of scripture, theology, church history, science, and physiology in meditation. As with other spiritual practices that I've begun (like observing sabbath), I've learned that the *why* of something sustains the *how*. Why meditate—why not just pray? These chapters unpack that question and are centered on Jesus' meditation practice, as well as empirical, data-driven evidence of the benefits of establishing a meditation practice in a nonstop world. Chapter four outlines the daily structure and format of the meditation practice, explaining the purpose of each part of the process.

In chapter five, I explain each meditation method in depth, offering you the tools for your forty-day meditation practice. These forty days mirror Jesus' journey through the wilderness, and they contain eight days of practice per meditation type. Each daily practice contains a freedom statement, an opening and closing ritual, brief directions for the practice, and prompts adapted from the Ignatian Examen for journaling. The order of each meditation method is purposeful, helping you build your knowledge and confidence. Try each meditation method sequentially—at least your first time through the book. Even if you encounter a method you don't like or find helpful, pay attention to the *why* of your aversion. Record your responses to the daily Examen practice. What gets measured gets managed; the struggles (like my wrestling for six days with the meditation app) are useful in understanding and experiencing your spiritual growth.

Chapter six explores my own journey through this resource, which I had completed multiple times before this book ever reached your hands. In that chapter, I describe what happened to me as I embraced a meditation practice—beginning with trauma nightmares and hesitations, outlining my challenges, wins, and setbacks—and share where I am now. This chapter serves as a reminder of the real, striving, and struggling human behind this book, who walks alongside you on this journey. You are not alone; you and I are beginners together.

Chapter seven gives you the opportunity to reflect on your own forty-day journey. This chapter includes questions for you, scenarios you may have run into, and suggestions to assist you in continuing your meditation practice. This book is meant to be used repeatedly, and you may choose to write your thoughts directly in the book or in a separate journal to document your progress. Finally, the appendix provides an at-a-glance description of each meditation method as well as additional *lectio divina* readings and meditation resources.

Group Settings

This book can easily be used in group settings. When using it with others, however, encourage members to take turns teaching and leading the group. Otherwise, it's easy to fall into the trap I'd been stuck in for years—being the teacher instead of the student. Here are some ways to utilize this book effectively with others:

Family. I encourage you to use this book as a family and/or with your spouse if that will help you stay accountable to the practice. In fact, this book could be used intergenerationally—with children or older adults—to listen for God and cope with modern-day stress. For the youngest members of your family, you may need to simplify some concepts, but don't hesitate to involve children. Through teaching and leading many workshops on sabbath and meditation, I've observed that children enjoy learning different spiritual practices and are often more receptive to them than adults. Children have much to teach us.

Each daily practice can be done as a family, but encourage your family members to keep the silence during the actual practice so that you don't distract one another. Pick a time of day that works for everyone and doesn't cause unnecessary stress, and agree on a time limit for your meditation. The leader should remind family members of the meditation method for the day. Set a timer and practice silently, keeping the time especially short if involving little ones. Afterward, feel free to answer the Examen questions as a group or write your responses privately and determine if you want to share.

Faith-Based, Congregational Small Group. Because a forty-day journey comprises this book, it can be used during liturgical seasons (Advent, Lent, Eastertide, or Ordinary Time). It also can be used in ways that correspond with cultural and societal celebrations and events—New Year's resolutions, a summer spiritual practice series, or a kick-off to the academic year. Below is a sample outline that includes ample time to discuss the chapters and two weeks of practice. Alternatively, the group can meet the first week to introduce the concept and discuss chapters one through four and meet each subsequent week to check in on the week's practice. I encourage you to schedule a debriefing session after the forty days to discuss what you have learned.

OPTION ONE

Week 1: Invitation to the Book (Read chapter one before the first meeting.)

Week 2: The Theology and Science of Meditation (Discuss chapters two and three.)

Week 3: Introduction to the Forty-Day Journey (Discuss chapter four; consider your curiosities and anticipations for the journey.)

Week 4: Practice Method One (Breath Meditation). Check in with your group. How did the week go? Share and discuss your responses to the Daily Examen and prepare for Method Two (Centering Meditation).

Week 5: Your Journey (Discuss chapters six and seven.) What happened in your fourteen days of practice (Breath and Centering Meditation)? What challenged you? What energized you?

Optional Week 6: Continue to practice, debrief, and discuss.

OPTION TWO

Week 1: Briefly discuss chapters one through four (members will have read those chapters before coming to the first meeting). Discuss Method One (Breath Meditation). How did it go? What challenged/energized you?

Week 2: Discuss Method Two (Centering Meditation). How did it go? What challenged/energized you?

Week 3: Discuss Method Three (*Lectio Divina* Meditation). How did it go? What challenged/energized you?

Week 4: Discuss Method Four (Loving-Kindness Meditation). How did it go? What challenged/energized you?

Week 5: Discuss Method Five (Devotional Meditation). How did it go? What challenged/energized you? Briefly discuss remaining chapters (six and seven) and your plan for moving forward with a meditation practice.

Book Club (Faith-Based or Not). Most book clubs read a book and then meet to discuss it. You can certainly use this traditional method, but be sure to give your club enough time to complete the forty-day journey. Or you could divide the book (and your meetings) in two: Meet first to discuss chapters one through four. For your next meeting (after at least forty days), meet to discuss how the practice went, as well as chapters six and seven. Your group may choose to read another book in between to give everyone time to get through the forty-day portion. A good companion book to this one is *For Sabbath's Sake: Embracing Your Need for Rest, Worship, and Community* (Upper Room Books, 2017).

Before You Begin

Before you begin this book—whether on your own or with your family, your Sunday school class, small group, or book club, ponder these questions and write your responses in your book or in a journal.

1. What led you to choose this book? What was your motivation for wanting to explore meditation? If this book was chosen for you by someone else, why do you think God brought this practice into your life at this time?

2. Consider the stressors in your life. What makes your mind, body, and spirit feel cluttered, disconnected, and overwhelmed? Imagine how practicing silence and listening for God might help.

3. Does being still and listening to God come naturally to you? Why or why not?

4. Name any resistance you feel to beginning this practice (skepticism, theological conviction, uncertainty, doubt, reluctance, frustration, resentment, and so on).

5. Describe your curiosity about meditation.

6. Name your intention for beginning this practice. How might your relationship with God, yourself (your body, mind, and spirit), and others deepen, grow, and benefit from this practice?

Chapter Two

THE CASE FOR MEDITATION

The Lord *passed by, and a great and strong wind rent the mountains, and brake in pieces the rocks before the* Lord; *but the* Lord *was not in the wind: and after the wind an earthquake; but the* Lord *was not in the earthquake: And after the earthquake a fire; but the* Lord *was not in the fire: and after the fire a still small voice.*

—1 Kings 19:11-12, KJV

In the morning, while it was still very dark, [Jesus] got up and went out to a deserted place, and there he prayed.

—Mark 1:35

The *why* of something sustains the *how*.

Once we finish mandatory K–12 education, we enter the world of discovering our own *whys* and *hows*. Prior to then, our parents, our guardians, our caregivers, the state, or federal law determine our *why*, creating an environment or condition not of our own choosing.

"But *why?*" we asked as kids when we didn't want to go to bed, go to school, or obey the rules.

"Because I said so," our parent, guardian, caregiver, or judicial system responded.

When we enter adulthood, the *why* of something becomes *our* responsibility. No law, job, diet, schooling, or spiritual practice can be kept and sustained unless we know (consciously or unconsciously) *why* we are doing it. *Why* not break the law? We don't want to lose our freedom. *Why* keep showing up to that job? We must pay the rent, keep the lights on, and feed the kids. *Why* modify our diets? To avoid illness, taking medication, chronic disease—or maybe just to fit into those skinny jeans. *Why* earn our GEDs or attend college or trade school? We crave better opportunities. *Why* keep a spiritual practice? That's a tougher question.

After my attempt at implementing a meditation practice with a popular app became a free-association Google search in my brain, I knew I was going in the wrong direction. I also knew that I wouldn't give meditation an authentic and enthusiastic try until I discovered *why* I needed and wanted to meditate. "Because my therapist said so" was not enough motivation for me. Had it been, I would have stayed the course with Mr. Villain Narrator, despite my petty aversion to his voice.

Like any other behavior, career, diet, degree, or spiritual path we pursue, the *reason* perpetuates the everyday habit. But many of our *whys* are fear-based: We want to avoid loss, pain, and suffering, so we keep the law, the job, the diet, and attend the classes. But I didn't want to pursue a meditation practice just because I feared the trauma nightmares following my mother's death. That motivation would have been short-term and short-lived. I needed the long-term, sustainable *why* of meditation before I could pursue the *how*. *Why* should anyone—especially Christians—meditate? Aside from a doctor telling us to, what is the greater spiritual reason? Does meditation have spiritual and theological value? Is it prescribed in scripture? How does it differ from prayer?

As a meditation skeptic, I needed to take a deep dive into this ancient-practice-turned-modern-craze. I needed to ask questions and to study meditation from a biblical, historical, theological, and evidence-based perspective to be convinced of its utility for Christians. And like the good Sunday-school student that I was, I remembered that the answer to every question begins with "Jesus!" So that's where I started.

Jesus Meditates?

The Bible contains no shortage of writings on Jesus' contemplative life. From direction for solitary prayer (see Matthew 6:6), to Jesus' prayer at his baptism (see Luke 3:21), to teaching communal prayer (see Matthew 6:9-13), and to Jesus' fervent prayers for himself before his crucifixion (see Matthew 26:39, 42, 44), the Gospels make a compelling case that spiritual practice is central to Jesus' life and ministry. Jesus seeks the "deserted place[s]" (Mark 1:35) for solitary prayer, prays for his followers (see John 17), and even teaches his disciples how to pray for their enemies (see Matthew 5:44-45).

Throughout the New Testament, Jesus juxtaposes his *exterior* life—his ministry and service to others, his relationships with his disciples—and his *interior* one. This explains why Paul, in writing some of the first letters to Jesus' followers, asks them to pray without ceasing (see Thessalonians 5:17) and to be in prayer about everything (see Philippians 4:6). Prayer—or talking *with* God silently or aloud—about a topic (thanksgiving, praise, confession, supplication, and intercession) is crucial to our understanding of the historical Jesus, Jesus as the

Messiah, the Trinity, and the subsequent development of the early church. Prayer provides the cornerstone of the Christian faith.

But did Jesus *meditate?* And if so, how was his meditation practice different from his prayer life? What would *meditation* have meant to him as a Jewish reformer living in the first century?

Meditation in Scripture

The modern English term we know as *meditate* originates from the Latin word *meditatio,* from the verb *meditari,* meaning "to think or reflect upon."[1] Did Jesus *think and reflect* upon God the Father, his call to ministry, his service to others, his friendships, his death, and what was to come? Absolutely. The scriptural examples of Jesus meditating as defined above—both in community and in solitude—demonstrate an intentional man who thought and reflected deeply on God and God's will. The private, contemplative garden of Gethsemane scene in particular, which appears in all three synoptic Gospels (Matthew, Mark, and Luke), provides insight into Jesus' meditation on his forthcoming crucifixion. (See Matthew 26:39; Mark 14:35-36; and Luke 22:42.)

In my own prayer life, which I discussed in chapter one, I found myself being a "Chatty Cathy," employing formulas and checklists that didn't leave much room for *listening* to God. Jesus' spiritual practices—including his meditation—by contrast, don't include dissertation-length demands on God. Rather, Jesus prays (and teaches others to pray) simply and reverently. He also teaches his students to fervently *meditate* (think or reflect upon) on God's commandments, given to them through the Jewish canon.

Mother Mary and Joseph raised Jesus in the ancient faith of Judaism, which developed among God's chosen people following God's covenant with Abram (see Genesis 15), who later received the name *Abraham* in Genesis 17. Jewish scripture (known as the Old Testament in Christianity) is composed of twenty-four books written in Hebrew called the *TANAKH,* an acronym for *Torah* (teachings or law—the five books attributed to Moses), *Nevi'im* (the prophets' writings), and *Ketuvim* (the wisdom writings).[2] As a devout Jewish boy, Jesus was steeped deeply in Hebrew scriptures. We know this because, on the cusp of his teenage years, his parents lose him for three days during a temple pilgrimage to Jerusalem. When they finally find him, he is sitting among the temple priests and teachers, asking questions and learning. (See Luke 2:41-51.)

In the *TANAKH,* the root of the Hebrew word for meditate is *hagah,* which means "to sigh, murmur, or ponder."[3] *Hagah* is used throughout Hebrew scriptures but perhaps most famously in Psalm 1:2 as a verb: "Their delight is in the law of the LORD, and on his law they meditate [*yeheggeh*] day and night." In 70 CE, when the *TANAKH* was translated into

Greek—called *The Septuagint* (Greek for "seventy")—*hagah* became *meletao*, meaning "to ponder or study."[4, 5, 6] Centuries after the Christian church is established and is utilizing both *The Septuagint* and the Greek New Testament, the biblical canon undergoes another major translation into Latin. *The Vulgate*—the translation of those Hebrew and Greek texts into the Latin Bible—is widely disseminated in the sixteenth century. The use of the derivative of *meditari* is found in *The Vulgate*, which later yielded the English *meditate*.[7]

Meditation, then, considering both its modern definition and its Hebrew and Greek uses in scripture, would not have been an unusual practice for Jesus. He was raised in a faith that taught its followers to *yeheggeh* (meditate) on scripture day and night. The story of Jesus as a young boy in the temple reminds me that Jesus was indeed part of a religious tradition that viewed contemplating scripture and God as essential practices of spirituality.

Eastern Traditions: Hinduism and Buddhism

The term, essence, and practice of *meditation*, however, even precedes Judaism, the *TANAKH*, Jesus' life and ministry, *The Septuagint,* the Greek New Testament, and *The Vulgate*. It is a deeply rooted spiritual practice of the ancient Eastern traditions of Hinduism (developed circa 2,000 BCE). From Hinduism, Buddhism is birthed circa 600 BCE; both traditions are indigenous to India. Hinduism is the world's oldest living global religious tradition, preceding Judaism by a few centuries. In Hinduism, meditation is called *dhyana* (pronounced "dyaan"). Sacred Hindu texts describe *dhyana* as an uninterrupted flow of attention toward the object of meditation.[8] *Dhyana* is the seventh of the eight limbs of yoga (the Hindu spiritual lifestyle—not the group exercise class). *Dhyana* is only achieved after the practitioner has completed the first six stages of yoga, which include spiritual practices like *ahimsa* (nonviolence), calming material and sensual desires, breaking the mind's habit of being pulled away by its endless deluge of thoughts, and cultivating concentration.[9]

Hindus believe that only when attention becomes uninterrupted can a person become fully absorbed in something—and, in the case of meditation, that something is God. According to the *Yoga-Sutras of Patanjali*, we cannot attain this state of *dhyana* until our chaotic minds and senses have been reined in. For Hindus, authentic *dhyana* (meditation) has only been achieved when our mind is fixated on God—or the object of our meditation—without distraction.[10] In contrast, the Abrahamic texts and faiths of Judaism and Christianity place less overt focus on freeing ourselves from desires *before* attempting to concentrate on God. Still, the ethos of meditation remains: a flow of attention and concentration that allows us to deeply think and reflect on the object of our meditation, which, in the case of the Abrahamic faiths, is also God.

Gazing at God

In one of the earliest forms of Christianity—called Orthodox Christianity—*hesychasm* is the mystical tradition of contemplative prayer. In Orthodox hesychasm, the goal of contemplative practice is *theoria*, Greek for "gazing."[11] Orthodox Christians use icons (small images of Christ and the Holy Family depicted on wood or other materials) to practice hesychasm. In this way, icons are often called "windows to God." "Gazing at God" and the use of icons may be unfamiliar to Protestants, who do not regularly use such visual elements in their spiritual practice. But hesychasm helps us naturally quiet our environments and our minds to concentrate on God. Similarly, in the *bhakti-yoga* tradition of Hinduism, intense devotion (gazing) and worship of God through meditation is achieved through repeating the names of God (*mantras*) on a rosary-like strand of beads called *japa mala*. Meditating on these names helps displace the mind's wandering and yearning for material desires, culminating in love for God (*bhakti*).

But how often do we embrace time to sit silently and "gaze" at God in our mind's eye? How often do we think and reflect deeply on scripture and the names and attributes of God? What might hesychasm look like in the life of a Protestant Christian who has only known formulaic prayers and long lists of prayer requests? I've never stood at the edge of the Grand Canyon, but when I imagine the experience of seeing it for the first time, I think of awe. I envision myself staring silently at this natural wonder, gazing at it for hours to think and reflect on its beauty and mysticism. In my imagination, I don't see or hear myself prattling on to myself or the tourist next to me about how great it is, wasting air on a description that cannot live up to its reality. Instead, I am speechless (a rarity), taking only deep breaths amid such indescribable sacred wonder. This awe and wonder *are* hesychasm—gazing lovingly at the One who is indescribably awesome, such that we cannot pull our eyes away. When practiced well and over time, this uninterrupted flow of wordless concentration allows us to be still and quiet enough to *feel* the presence of God.

Early Christianity: The Development of Contemplative Practices

The official, institutional Christian church emerged several hundred years after Jesus' death and resurrection. Prior to this, the earliest Christian communities began with Easter's resurrection miracle, first seen and heard by Mary Magdalene and later shared with the disciples, after which the "good news" continued to spread. (See John 20:1-18.) But Christianity was not a welcome religious practice in the Roman Empire; its counterculturalism was met with disdain, persecution, and, ultimately, martyrdom. As a result, Christianity developed underground, unwedded to the state, until the conversion of Emperor Constantine, who became the religion's most popular (and, in addition to Paul, its most important) convert. By 321 CE,

Constantine declared Christianity and its practices permittable in the public square. By 380 CE, Sunday became the Roman Empire's official and mandated day of rest, thus declaring Christianity its official religion.

While Emperor Constantine's conversion, enthusiasm, and power were considered a boon to building, growing, and preserving the Christian church, there were downsides to becoming official and prevalent. The early church became more complex, with growing numbers of adherents, the acquisition of buildings for public worship, and treasuries. With money and prestige came more to look after and protect. Christianity became enmeshed with the state and politics, suffocating the opportunity to stand in contrast to the dominant culture.[12] With less emphasis on the basics, like deep spirituality and discipleship, many Christians fought against this turn from authentic practice to material gain and prosperity. This, in turn, led Christianity away from the idea that persecuted martyrs were the ideal embodiment of Christian life and discipleship toward the establishment of monastics (from the Greek word *monos,* meaning "alone" or "solitary").[13] Monks, who rejected church wealth and materialism, became the symbol of foundational Christian practices. In their protest of what the public church had become, they withdrew from society to restore the former countercultural spiritual practices of Christianity and to pursue holiness. These first monastics valued meditative spiritual disciplines over public worship that had and would continue to become the beating heart of a church welcomed in the public sphere.

According to Saint Athanasius, one of Christianity's earliest writers and theologians, Egyptian hermit Saint Antony is viewed as Christianity's very first monastic.[14] In Athanasius's *The Life of Antony,* written circa 357 CE, Saint Antony's solitary and meditative lifestyle became popular as the monastic standards of the fourth-century church. Subsequent Christian men and women also felt called to withdraw from a public Christianity they perceived as becoming more corrupt so that they could embody the prayerful, contemplative life of service found in Christ's teachings. *Anchorites*, from the Greek *anchoresis* ("to withdraw") also became a staple of the Christian monastic tradition. Medieval Christianity's Julian of Norwich became the most well-known anchoress, whose influence on Christian spirituality is still prevalent today.[15]

When individual monastics withdrew from society, they eventually formed communities through which they shared common life, work, fellowship, and spiritual practice under a common rule. While Pachomius (c. 292–346 CE) is credited with founding communal monasticism, Saint Benedict of Nursia (480–550 CE) authored what later became the influential *Rule of St. Benedict,* which many intentional Christian communities and monastics keep today.[16] The "rule" established a balanced rhythm for individual monks and the community. It rooted practitioners in daily contemplation through shared liturgical prayer, mindful manual labor, and *lectio divina*—which includes meditation on the sacred scriptures.[17] *Lectio divina* is a form of meditation that focuses on listening to sacred scriptures and then reflecting and responding to what God invites us to hear. The earliest Christian monastics used all 150 Psalms as the foundation of their contemplative practices, including *lectio divina*. Meditating on the Psalms was a way to create opportunities to "gaze at" God.

This strong evidence for the return to ancient contemplative practices by the earliest Christian monastics—who sought to restore the authentic teachings and practices of Jesus amid a religion going the way of materialism and world—encourages me to do the same. In an era of "nones" and "dones," many Christians are "finished" with the church as they—or their parents and grandparents—have known it. I'm not saying that we should board up church buildings and call it a day, but I do think millennials (born in the early 1980s) and Generation Z (born in the late 1990s and into the 2000s) are sending this message: They crave authentic practices and true community, which isn't necessarily found in steepled, auditorium, or coffee-shop churches with electric guitars and praise-band music. In many ways, the church reform movement that awaits us could be as simple as leaving behind the literal and metaphorical institutional "stuff" to return to the basics. Just as the desert monastics reclaimed the contemplative roots of spiritual practice based on the meditative example of the Psalms and Jesus, we can do the same.

Mystics and Merton

The desert monastics made a compelling case for meditation—in its scriptural sense of deep thinking and reflection—for early Christianity. Later, the Orthodox Christian hesychasm tradition of "gazing," as well as the medieval mystics like Julian of Norwich and Teresa of Ávila, continued to build on the practices from the early desert mothers and fathers, rooting themselves in practices focused on listening for God and experiencing God's presence. One of these prominent practices was the "Jesus Prayer," which emerged from the anonymously written *The Way of the Pilgrim*. This prayer, which is "Lord, Jesus Christ, Son of God, have mercy on me, a sinner," became another tool for "gazing" meditation and deep reflection and contemplation on God and God's attributes. The anonymous pilgrim who penned the book repeated this prayer on his journey as a way of engaging in ceaseless prayer. (See 1 Thessalonians 5:17.) Participation in hesychasm fixes our attention on God.

For modern Protestant Christians, these practices may seem obscure. Thomas Merton (1915–68), the well-known Trappist monk and priest, helped make contemplative practices mainstream for American practitioners. But Merton was careful to mark the distinction between prayer and meditation. Merton wrote that through meditation, we hear God "in the depths of our own being: for we ourselves are words of His."[18] For Merton, meditation provided a conduit for hearing this echo of God. He believed that the contemplative practice of listening leads us to "a deep resonance in the inmost center of our spirit in which our very life loses its separate voice and resounds with the majesty and the mercy of the Hidden and Living One. [God] answers Himself in us and this answer is new life, divine creativity, making all things new."[19] Like the ancient monastics and medieval mystics, Merton connected meditation to the interior contemplative life—one in which our attention moves from us to God.

The Meditation Fallacy

While many modern Christians claim meditation to be off limits in their own spiritual practice, there's no need to disregard, throw out, or diminish an ancient tool that early, medieval, and even twentieth-century Christians found vital to their faith. Early Christians embraced Jesus' contemplative nature and incorporated such integral tools as meditation on the Psalms, *lectio divina*, and, later, hesychasm, *theoria*, and the Jesus Prayer into their spiritual lives. But there is a key difference between these Christian practices and what has become the twenty-first-century prayer model.

Today, most Christians pray as a way to hold space for what they need to *tell* God. Meditation, on the other hand, holds space for what God needs to "tell" us. In our prayers, we confess to, praise, invoke, and supplicate God. In our meditation, we *listen* for God—whether it's through the Spirit, scripture, or even mystically in ways we cannot explain with our limited language and finite brains. This is not to say that we do not listen for or discern God's movement in prayer, but I do believe our tendency (at least mine) is for prayer to be "loud," focusing on ourselves rather than quietly listening for that "still small voice" (1 Kings 19:12, KJV) or for the subtle, sacred ways God shows up around and within us—even through our own breath. While prayer can be wordless—"The Spirit helps us in our weakness; for we do not know how to pray as we ought, but that very Spirit intercedes with sighs too deep for words" (Rom. 8:26)—we tend to use prayer as a way to push our needs, confessions, agendas, formulas, requests, and lists. It puts *us* in the center. Meditation—the listening counterpart to prayer—recalibrates us to the triune God, who is the rightful center.

Meditation allows for a certain kind of fixed attention in which we can experience God's presence as close as our own breath, which Job reminds us is "the breath of the Almighty" (33:4). For me, meditation has meant tuning out my own agenda in order to tune in to God's. But less chatter and more listening for God does not come naturally for me. I, along with many Christians, view prayer as my opportunity to talk God's ear off about everything. And that's not how Jesus or the early Christians understood their connection to God. Instead, they grounded their spirituality in meditation—thinking deeply, reflecting, gazing, and fixing their attention in order to listen for God's stirrings within and around them. In my own life, I haven't held much space for experiencing God in this way.

Prayer is at the heart of Christianity, both ancient and modern, and there is nothing wrong with that. But I believe that meditation is *different* from prayer. They are two distinct and useful tools. We tend to overuse prayer and neglect the quiet practices of reflecting on the Psalms or utilizing *lectio divina.* Most of us have never heard of the ancient Christian practice of hesychasm, *theoria,* or fixing our attention on God through the Jesus Prayer. Our noisy culture inclines us to practice a lopsided faith that keeps our focus on *us.* We've developed ways and methods of prayer that work but aren't necessarily balanced with cultivating deep contemplation to discern God's presence, voice, and guidance. For those of us with talkative natures, our minds constantly racing, prayer can turn into a lot of words and not much listening.

Sitting Chickens

"Meditation is not sitting like a chicken," the Tibetan monk told the gathered Buddhists. They erupted in nervous laughter, but their soft giggles couldn't compete with his boisterous guffaws. I was a stranger among them, invited by a dear Buddhist friend, Heather, to observe the Sunday morning *dharma,* or teaching. I didn't recall seeing chickens sit, but I hadn't been near poultry recently. Perhaps he meant "sitting duck"? It'd be an easy idiom to confuse. In English, a "sitting duck" is someone who puts himself or herself in a vulnerable position due to lack of attention to what is happening in the environment around him or her.

In this Tibetan monk's line of thinking, the Buddhists who'd gathered that morning to learn about meditation were all "sitting chickens," unknowing prey to rapacious thoughts, waiting to pounce. But when we minimize the distractions in our mind, the monk added, we are happier, better people. We become less self-absorbed and more concerned with the world beyond ourselves. As likely the only Christian clergyperson in the room, I translated his message through the lens of my own tradition: When we can be mindfully aware of and attentive to God's presence, we are less likely to be spiritually slaughtered by our fixation with the constant, egocentric nattering of a 24/7 society.

We know meditation works scripturally, historically, and theologically, but can it shore us up against the "prey" of chaos? How does meditation affect our brains and bodies, which, in turn, shape and form our spirituality through the mind-body-spirit connection? This next chapter explores how meditation—particularly our God-given breath—keeps our bodies, brains, and spirits in balance, protecting us from the metaphorical dangers of being "sitting chickens."

Chapter Three

THE POWER OF BREATH

Inhale, and God approaches you. Hold the inhalation, and God remains with you. Exhale, and you approach God. Hold the exhalation, and surrender to God.

—Krishnamacharya

Just as you do not know how the breath comes to the bones in the mother's womb, so you do not know the work of God, who makes everything.

—Ecclesiastes 11:5

In the modern world, we encounter no shortage of stimuli vying for our attention. From the 24/7 market economy to the initiation of technology-as-appendages, this is an era of see, be, and do more—now. Nicholas Carr, author of *The Shallows: What the Internet Is Doing to Our Brains,* writes that the typical smartphone user (which is 77 percent of Americans, according to The Pew Research Center) checks his or her phone nearly eighty times per day—that is, at least 30,000 times per year.[1,2] The smartphone, even amid the TV, personal computer, and tablet, has won the race for the strongest technological brain magnet. Though portable electronic devices have leveled the playing field of information access, they also have become a constant source of aggressive, dopamine-driven software engineering. Incessant notifications have trained us to crave what every gadget has to offer.

In his *Wall Street Journal* article "How Smartphones Hijack Our Brains," Carr cites numerous studies that demonstrate how the mere presence—even when not in use—of a smartphone drains our brain's cognitive resources, making it more difficult to concentrate and problem solve. In addition to the brain drain, Carr writes that smartphones also breed anxiety, or "ringxiety" as some call it. Studies show that when we don't immediately respond to or check a smartphone's ping, ring, or vibration, our blood pressure and heart rates spike.[3]

Our ancestors faced their own stressors—predators, violence, war, and industrial and technological advancements, for better or worse. But the smartphone is unique because it is glued to us twenty-four hours a day—even while we sleep—and vies for our waking attention at least eighty times per day. With a smartphone ever at the ready, making time for quiet and thoughtful meditation can be a Sisyphean climb. It's no wonder spiritual practices have been squeezed out; it's tough to compete with such a powerful brain magnet.

Gambler's Fallacy

How have we become so addicted to stimulation that sitting quietly by ourselves to think and reflect is nearly impossible? David Greenfield, psychologist and assistant professor of psychiatry at the University of Connecticut, says the coding used in smartphone engineering is based on the same premise as Ivan Pavlov's famous dog study as well as the science behind slot machines. Like Pavlov's dogs, the pings and vibration of the smartphone's notification system trigger our brain to release dopamine, signaling pleasure. But until we check the phone, we don't know what the content of the message will be: Will it be good (a text from a loved one), bad (an angry email from our boss), or indifferent (a notification about the weather)? It's the same trick, Greenfield says, used to hook gamblers on slot machines.[4]

We check our phone over and over—no matter what—because every so often, we receive a *desired* text, email, or social media like/comment/follow. Checking our devices has become analogous to playing the slot machine; we're always hoping for a win. When we do experience an actual or metaphorical jackpot—no matter how big or small—we want to keep playing, even after subsequent losses, because previous experience tells us that a victory is not far away. Scientifically, this is called a variable ratio schedule of reinforcement. The results from the smartphone or the slot machine are always random, but that randomness increases our urge to check the device or play just in case that desired outcome is waiting for us.[5]

In the critical thinking course I teach to community college students, we learn about these kinds of flaws in human reasoning. This one is called the "gambler's fallacy." It means that a past event has an impact on our skilled judgment and observation (or not) of a current random event.[6] But just because a random event has occurred before, what should our logic actually tell us? How many times do we actually *have* that winning text, email, social media notification, or jackpot waiting for us? Though the odds are small, it's enough to make us neglect reason and check—just in case—nearly eighty times per day. By doing so, we continue to feed the flawed thinking that a ping, beep, or vibration will pay off more than it disrupts our cognitive work and spiritual growth.

What Happens in Vegas Can Be Cured by Vagus

I've never been to Las Vegas. My loved ones tell me that I'd hate it—too much stimulation, lights, noise, and smoke and no differentiation between day and night. Though I've never *experienced* Vegas, I think many of us bring Sin City into our ordinary lives. I imagine our brains and bodies behaving like Las Vegas tourists: darting in and out of casinos with their blinking neon signs. The "casinos" of our lives are the multiple Internet browser tabs we have open on our computer screens and the apps we gawk at continuously, waiting for the jackpot. We pop back and forth from one virtual task to another, on the search for the next dopamine hit, because our experience tells us that we've "won" before and we can "win" again. We convince ourselves that we can handle the multitasking, the distractions, and the information overload. Instead, we're drained—because "Vegas" all day, every day is exhausting.

This overstimulation is not good for our bodies, which are woven together beautifully by a complex system of muscles, bones, connective tissues, and, most importantly, our nerves, which carry messages throughout our body. The homeostasis and operation of our insides are controlled by the autonomic nervous system, which is composed of two parts: the sympathetic division and the parasympathetic division. In total, these two systems regulate our blood pressure, heart rate, body temperature, breathing, digestion, metabolism, water balance, production of body fluids, as well as our bathroom habits and sexual responses.[7] However, these two divisions play opposing roles. The sympathetic division is the "fight-or-flight" system. It prepares our bodies for urgent situations by increasing our heart rate and blood pressure, dilating our pupils, and raising our oxygen intake by opening our airways and increasing our breathing rate. It diverts blood to the heart, diaphragm, lungs, and muscles and away from nonessential organs, readying us to fight or flee. In contrast, the parasympathetic division is the "relaxation response." It slows the heart rate, lowers the blood pressure, relaxes airway muscles, returning the airway to its normal width, and stimulates our routine digestion and urination.[8]

Each division of the autonomic nervous system releases chemicals into the body. The sympathetic system secretes norepinephrine, while the parasympathetic releases acetylcholine. The vagus nerve, which is one of the longest nerves in the body, wanders (*vagus* is Latin for "wandering") from the skull, through the chest, and down to the abdomen. The vagus is unique in that it carries signals in both directions, from the heart, muscles, digestive system, and organs to the brain and vice versa. In fact, through its connection to the lungs, diaphragm, and gut, the vagus nerve has the most input from external stimuli of any nerve.

Why Vagus Is Your Best Friend

So what does the vagus nerve have to do with meditation? The deep, rhythmic breathing of meditation and slow diaphragm movement stimulates the vagus nerve, releasing acetylcholine and counteracting the fight-or-flight response of the sympathetic nervous system.[9] Stimulating the vagus nerve with slow breathing is not a new phenomenon. In the ancient yoga tradition of *pranayama*, deep, controlled breathing has been and is used to reach meditative states by regulating the breath and, thus, calming the autonomic nervous system. After yoga and its philosophy arrived in the United States in the 1800s and its popularity grew in the mid-1900s, breath control became a part of a holistic approach to overall wellness.[10]

Typically, humans breathe ten to twenty times per minute; "slow" breathing is considered four to ten respirations per minute. Normal respiration is called "tidal breathing," which means that during consistent inspiration (inhale) and expiration (exhale), the body receives a normal "tidal volume" of oxygen to circulate within the respiratory and cardiovascular systems. Tidal breathing is controlled by a group of muscles called the "respiratory pump," which includes the diaphragm. These muscles all work passively most of the time—that is, without our knowing or effort. However, when our breathing becomes purposeful, the effort of controlling it activates these muscles more. Optimal respiration includes this activated regulation of the diaphragm such that on the inhale, the belly appears to expand, while the ribs stay low and move laterally. For those who have sung in a choir, this is how the choir director wants singers to breathe. Active breathing effort increases our tidal volume (the more oxygen we have use of within our body). Slow respirations—that is, six breaths per minute—maximize ventilation and reduce any waste in oxygen.[11]

The medulla oblongata, located along the base of the brain stem, is the body's "neural pacemaker."[12] It controls the body's involuntary cardiac and respiratory functions such that without it, we would not live. It also aids in transferring messages from the brain to the nervous system and back. Each arm of the autonomic nervous system (sympathetic and parasympathetic) is controlled by the central respiratory center in the brain.[13] As stated, the autonomic nervous system exerts opposing control over the heart and respiratory pumps. The sympathetic is our "stress" system, sending signals to release norepinephrine when we need it, while the parasympathetic excretes soothing chemicals. The parasympathetic system, surprisingly, has a faster influence on the heart and lungs because of the length and power of the vagus nerve. As humans learn to slow their breathing voluntarily (reducing the number of breaths per minute from twelve or sixteen to ten), we begin to exert control over vagal activity and augment its effects. Over time, strengthening our vagal activity has been shown to shift the body toward parasympathetic dominance, but it requires at least three months of sustained slow breathing practice to do so.[14]

Though the vagus is a nerve, we can imagine it as a muscle that, when exercised by slow breathing, can be strengthened such that our "friendly" parasympathetic system takes the lead, minimizing the sympathetic activity that keeps us on edge.[15] Not only does slow breathing minimize the body's need for sympathetic (fight-or-flight) chemicals, but also it helps our nervous system achieve balance, enhancing our autonomic parasympathetic (relaxation) response to physical and mental stressors.[16] In summary, slow breathing increases vagal activity, shifts the body toward parasympathetic dominance, augments vagal power, enhances modulation of sympathetic activities, and improves the body's autonomic responsiveness to stress.[17]

Take Six Deep Breaths

When my mother was ill for over two weeks, my sympathetic (flight-or-fight) nervous system launched into high gear, supplying my body with all the chemical resources I'd need to help my brother take care of her until the end. This constant overstimulation and release of norepinephrine led to medical trauma nightmares, a hallmark symptom of post-traumatic stress disorder. PTSD is caused by many circumstances, including the actual exposure or merely the threat of death and witnessing or learning about a close friend or family member's death.[18] In the days following my mother's death, when my therapist said, "You need to stop the automatic thinking," what she really meant was, "You need to calm down your sympathetic nervous system and balance it with the relaxation response of your parasympathetic nervous system by stimulating your vagus nerve." At the time, I wouldn't have been able to understand the complexity of my body's autonomic responses and its efforts to keep my body going during stressful circumstances. I didn't even know what the autonomic nervous system was and that meditation (deep breathing) had any real connection to it.

Once I realized the connection, I began to see evidence of it everywhere. In 2005, a Japanese study published in *Hypertension Research* of over 25,000 patients discovered something amazing about the correlation between blood pressure and deep breathing. In the study, researchers monitored the blood pressure readings of two groups of patients. Group DBG (Deep Breathing Group) was instructed to take six deep breaths at 80 percent capacity during a thirty-second rest in a chair; group CG (Control Group) was asked to sit quietly for thirty seconds, with no intentional directions given for breathing.[19]

Each group had its blood pressure taken before and after the thirty-second rest. The DBG had greater reductions in blood pressure than the CG—even after just half a minute. Though each group was given the same amount of time to sit quietly, the group that purposefully breathed deeply saw better circulatory results than those who merely sat for thirty seconds with no intentional deep breathing.[20] So, when we find ourselves in stressful situations where our sympathetic nervous system kicks in—with its blood pressure spikes and quickening pulse—people command us to "take a deep breath." Though their words may irritate us at the time, the advice is valid. These instructions are spot on for stimulating the vagus nerve—but it requires taking *six* deep breaths (or more) rather than one or two or four.

Because the vagus nerve is central to counteracting the sympathetic nervous system through deep breathing, most meditation practices (Eastern or Western, theistic or secular, Christian or otherwise) begin with the breath. The immediate calming of the body's natural stress responses frees the mind to focus its energy on something other than preparing for the primitive fight-or-flight response. Breathing is the foundation for any meditation modality because it provides the calming state through which we can receive what we need to hear or experience from God.

How, then, do we begin our meditation practice? One breath at a time.

Chapter Four

THE HOW OF MEDITATION

In the spiritual life there are no tricks and no short cuts.

—Thomas Merton

We need to find God, and [God] cannot be found in noise and restlessness. God is the friend of silence.

—Saint Teresa of Calcutta

I am not a work-in-progress person; I like *results*. Fast-forward me to the goal, please. I don't want to muddle through the minutia of working to achieve it. But worthwhile goals are not achieved in one day, nor without repetition. The same is true for establishing a solid spiritual practice. One day—or forty days—of meditation will not immediately transform us into Wilderness Jesus. A month of meditation does not yield a lotus-sitting Zen master unfazed by traffic, endless emails, or catastrophic life events. A meditation practice, however, will help us cultivate and deepen our spiritual lives, become closer to God, better understand how to live in the way of Christ, and be more equipped to cope with life's chaos. But practice is hard. We've all heard the saying "Practice makes perfect"—but whoever said it was wrong about the perfection part and right about practice.

Getting Started

Now that we have established meditation's scriptural, theological, cultural, and empirical value, we're ready to begin our forty-day journey. But how? One breath—and one day—at a time. This forty-day guided journey will help us stay the course in establishing a meditation routine. The book contains five methods of meditation: breath meditation, centering meditation, *lectio divina* meditation, loving-kindness meditation, and devotional meditation. We will practice each method for eight consecutive days. Learning five different methods of meditation will set us up well for continuing our meditation practice after the forty days are over. Each daily practice includes a freedom statement, an opening and closing ritual, a brief reminder of the day's meditation technique, and space for journaling using the Examen to record how the day's practice went.

Freeing Ourselves from Perfection—and Judgment

There is no wrong way to practice meditation. The daily meditation practices in this book emphasize the importance of offering ourselves freedom from judgment. Each day's meditation begins with a freedom statement unique to that day. The freedom statements free us from exactness and self-judgment. They also free us from other agendas and motivations so we can hold that day's intention during our practice. I developed these because I needed a daily reminder to celebrate learning and release myself from the belief that I could attain perfection. These freedom statements helped me remember my intention, purpose, and direction for the day. They encouraged me to free myself from unattainable perfection and concentrate instead on each day's progress and growth.

Just as our spiritual path and faith is unique to each of us, our meditation practice also is uniquely ours. A new spiritual practice requires patience to see how it unfolds. We needn't feel "behind" if we decide to spend more than the eight allotted days for each meditation method. And we needn't berate ourselves for feeling frustrated, bored, or anxious while learning a new practice. To remind ourselves of the progress we are making—no matter how small—I have included reflection questions with each day's practice. I used this space to process my meditation experience (Did I feel energized and peaceful or disconnected and frustrated?), to keep track of my progress, and to note how I felt God's presence. Journaling helps us discern what worked well and what didn't—and why.

When Do We Begin?

Any month, any day, and any time spent focusing on the breath and listening for God holds value. We needn't feel compelled to wait to begin a new spiritual practice until a certain day or liturgical season. This book can be used any time of year, but we may find that some months or liturgical seasons are especially conducive to turning inward and deepening the spiritual journey. For example, this book can be used as a New Year's resolution or during Lent, Advent and Christmastide (Advent plus the twelve days of Christmas is roughly forty days, depending upon the year), or Eastertide (the period after Easter until Pentecost is fifty days). The new year or beginning of an academic year are also good times to begin. Some may choose to start meditating during vacation when life feels less scheduled. These are merely suggestions; a meditation practice can begin on July 17, February 29, today, or tomorrow. However, I do suggest completing each of the forty days and not skipping days or meditation techniques. If I needed more time with a meditation method, I took it. Consistency is the toughest part of any spiritual practice. Even when I didn't feel like meditating, I made myself try it anyway. If I missed a day, I jumped back in the next day where I left off and kept going.

To start, I suggest that any meditation practice should last for no more than three to five minutes per day. By starting with a small amount of time, we increase our chances of "winning" and, therefore, are motivated to return to the practice the next day. Additionally, those three to five minutes can be *any* time during the day or night. For morning persons, start whenever the brain starts to kick in (for me, that is after drinking two cups of coffee and reading the previous day's *The Young and the Restless* recap). For night owls, use the five minutes before bedtime to power down from the day. Is lunchtime better? Try that. Afternoon? Go for it. Midnight while nursing the baby? Sounds good. Three in the morning during a break in your overnight work shift? No problem. There are *no restrictions*. Everyone and everything vie for our time; we can't beat ourselves up for not rising at 4:00 a.m. to keep monastic hours. That's not the goal. Thankfully, God is accessible at any hour and in any space.

The Basics of the Daily Practice

- **Finding the right time of day for your practice.** Only you know your schedule and any changes that might occur in it. If you are a weekend warrior in the retail, food, or service industries; a clergyperson; a night-shift worker; or a person who is on call for days at a time, you can adapt your practice to meet your needs. Here are some meditation times you may not have considered: early morning or midmorning during a coffee break; a few minutes during lunch; an afternoon walk; while waiting at an appointment or in school pickup line; while riding a bus, the subway, or another form of public transit. Or, if you can muster some deep breaths in moments of anxiety or anger during your day, go for it. When you can, keep the same daily meditation schedule. Once you determine the best time for you, set an alarm on your phone or in a digital or paper calendar. This will remind you of your daily appointment with yourself and God.
- **Amount of time.** I recommend starting with three minutes. When you're just beginning, three minutes is a surprisingly long time to meditate. You can work your way up to five, ten, fifteen minutes, and beyond. Starting small, however, ensures your success.

If three minutes feels too long—aim for one or two (seriously). Even *thirty seconds* of deep breathing has proven physiological benefits.

- **Be open to exploring all meditation methods.** You may dislike one of the five methods when you begin your practice. But keep practicing for eight days and be sure to include in your daily journaling *why* you disliked the method—was it frustrating, challenging, annoying, difficult, or stressful? If so, why? The data on what isn't working is just as important as the data on what is. It's all about growth.

Why Forty Days?

This journey is forty days for a reason. Scientifically, establishing a habit takes at least three weeks—or twenty-one days. Scripturally, the number forty has deep theological meaning. In her book, *Holy Listening with Breath, Body, and the Spirit,* author Whitney R. Simpson writes that forty is often associated with "times of testing and clarity in scripture. (See Genesis 7:12; Exodus 24:18; Matthew 4:2; and Acts 7:30.)"[1]

Tools Needed

As you move through your forty-day journey, you'll need a few tools, including this book, a timer, and a comfortable place to sit (a chair, a meditation cushion, the floor, an outdoor bench, a seat in a parked car, or an office desk) or a quiet place to stand, as well as a pen or pencil to journal using the Examen. This book and a writing utensil are completely portable, so don't limit yourself to indoors or the same place each day. Get creative; sit (or stand) anywhere you need to if it helps you keep this practice.

Common Threads for Each Meditation Method

You'll notice that several elements are included in each daily practice: a freedom statement, opening and closing rituals, and the daily Examen.

Freedom Statement

This book contains a freedom statement for each of the forty days. No two freedom statements are alike; each was crafted for a specific day of your journey. Use them to free yourself from judgment and perfection—but also use them to free yourself from any excuses, baggage, hesitations, and doubts you may have about meditation, sitting still, or listening for God. Some days I repeat the freedom statement several times—aloud or silently. Sometimes I write it on a sticky note and take it with me to work or place it in my car. Over time, the freedom statements have become a way to engage my muscle memory of letting go of perfection for that day. Use them however you'd like (repeat them as much as you need, print them out and place them where you can see them each day, take a photo and keep them on your phone—whatever works for you), but please use them each day.

Opening and Closing Rituals

The opening and closing rituals included in each day's meditation invite you to hold the space you are creating for yourself to think, to reflect, to gaze, and to be attentive. The opening ritual tells your body and mind that you are entering a sacred space. The closing ritual allows you to reenter the ordinary world—perhaps as someone with new insights and a sense of peace. The "Be Still" exercise, which uses Psalm 46:10, is short and easy to remember. For the opening ritual, begin with the entire verse, slowly removing words and phrases until you end with one word: *Be.*

Be still, and know that I am God.

Be still and know.

Be still.

Be.

For the closing ritual, begin with the single word *Be*, adding words and phrases until you have completed the original verse: "Be still, and know that I am God."

Be.

Be still.

Be still and know.

Be still, and know that I am God.

In this way, you complete the circle of space-holding, using scripture's call to stillness and noticing the presence of God.

Daily Examen

Saint Ignatius of Loyola lived in the fifteenth and sixteenth centuries and founded the Jesuit order of Catholicism. Ignatius believed that examining our ordinary, daily lives for God's presence draws us into a deeper relationship with the Trinity. He developed a rich meditative practice known as the Ignatian Examen. Today, the Examen takes many forms, but at its foundation lies a daily "check-in" with God and ourselves. The Examen concludes each day's practice. These questions invite and guide you to consider how your practice went that day. Feel free to write as little or as much as you want. Do write something—even if only a bullet point or two—as this will help you track your growth, including what's working and what's not.

For the Examen in this forty-day journey, I adapted the four-step process laid out in Sharon Seyfarth Garner's book *Mandalas, Candles, and Prayer: A Simply Centered Advent*. Garner emphasizes the intentional aspect of the Examen, which keeps you rooted in your life and forces you to stay present. Using her method, you'll neither dart too far into the future nor dwell too much in the past.

Here are the four guiding Examen questions for the end of your daily meditation:

1. **God's Presence.** How did you feel God's presence during this daily meditation, if at all? If you did not feel God's presence, write about why you think that might be.
2. **Gratitude.** Offer thanks to God for giving you the breath of life. Give thanks for the ways in which you felt God's presence before, during, and after your meditation. If you didn't feel God's presence, explore that. Write about gratitude for time to be still and silent and to devote a few minutes to your spiritual growth.
3. **Growth.** What challenged you today? What came easily today? Seek to grow from the moments during the meditation where you didn't feel connected to God, but also use this space to celebrate what went well. If you feel a barrier or block to God's presence, be aware of it or confess what might be going on. Additionally, take time to rejoice in what barriers or blockages were removed or lifted. Acknowledge what needs work and delight in improvement. Whether today's practice went smoothly or felt maddening, set the intention for tomorrow: "Tomorrow I will open myself to God's presence."
4. **Hope.** What do you hope tomorrow's meditation practice will bring? If today was challenging, what do you anticipate being less challenging tomorrow? What are you looking forward to? Focus on progress, not perfection.[2]

A Word about Fear of Emptying the Mind

Most people believe that meditation involves emptying the mind—a proposition that scares many Christians. They fear that this "emptying" provides an opening for the devil to pull up his RV and stay awhile. This book will *not* encourage you to empty your mind (that is nearly impossible, anyway). It will, however, invite you to calm and harness your mind without judgment—such that circuslike thoughts don't drag you away from your meditation practice. When you take hold of the leash—instead of letting your mind run wild—it's easier to focus your attention on God.

If this is a concern of yours, I invite you to release the "emptying the mind" roadblock used in so many Christian arguments against meditation. Instead, remember the use of meditation in scripture. Remember Jesus' contemplative practices and his desire to follow God's will. Remember the ancient Christian monastics, who used meditation to return to the roots of what Jesus modeled in scripture amid a growing institutionalization of the Christian faith. Most of all, trust that God will take care of you. "Consider the lilies," my mother always said, quoting that familiar verse from Luke 17 to bring me back to reality when I headed off the rails with unnecessary anxiety. Trust and invite God to join you on this journey so that you can gaze on God's presence. Hold on to your faith that says God is good and steadfast.

Tips for Beginning and Maintaining Your Christian Meditation Practice

1. Everyone can meditate—especially Christians. Upon hearing my Hindu and Buddhist friends discuss their dedicated meditation practices, I was the first to say, "I'd much rather be talking and praying" or "Christians don't typically do that." But these statements are not true. I *can* sit still and be quiet for at least three minutes, even if it's a struggle—and so can you. Historically, the earliest Christians practiced various forms of meditation. In scripture, Jesus ventures to a quiet place by himself to listen for God's will.

God created the breath that moves in and out of your body. Christian meditation is about using this life force to calm the mind and embrace silence to fill yourself with the awareness of God's presence. This book will lead you through meditating on God, God's scripture, and God's revelation of God's self. Meditation not only helps you listen for God to deepen your spiritual life and connect with God, yourself, and others but also possesses scientifically proven benefits for coping with stress and optimizing health.

2. Plan a time and place for your practice. Choose a time and place that is consistently quiet (and all yours if you are practicing by yourself). I've found that the time of day (or night) is more important than the space because available space often varies. Is your meditation time first thing in the morning? Is it on your coffee break, lunch break, or just before bed? I have a dear friend who practices in the carpool line for fifteen minutes while she waits to pick up her child from school. Is it during the bus or train ride before you go into work or return home? Schedule a time for meditation on your daily calendar. Set your phone alarm or an inexpensive battery-operated alarm clock (if you want to go low-tech like me) to remind yourself of your daily commitment.

You also can use that same device or a similar one (like a kitchen timer) to time your meditation practice, beginning with no more than three minutes. Because I prefer not to have my tempting smartphone around me, I use the timer on the stove in the morning. Start small—trust me, three minutes is *plenty* in the beginning. When you're ready, increase the time to five, ten, fifteen minutes, or beyond. By starting small, you set yourself up for success.

Protect those minutes—even when you don't feel like it. Consider them a date with God, something you would be remiss to bail on completely. Once you find your rhythm, those three minutes will give you the space to start, continue, or end your day with an awareness of God's presence.

3. Practice each meditation technique, even if you encounter one you don't like. The daily Examen will help you collect spiritual data about *why* you struggled with a specific method and what you might learn from it. I find that examining what's difficult is just as important as celebrating what came easily. God is present no matter what—amid the joy, frustrations, and growth. Once you've completed the entire cycle of forty days—and are thereby familiar with each practice—you may pick and choose what method works best for you. After the meditation app fiasco, I wanted to give up on breath meditation all together. Instead, I got rid of the app and started at the beginning (with the breath) and learned that this life force is the foundation for the other meditation techniques.

4. Grace yourself. This book is designed to give you a variety of tools with just enough guidance and accountability to help you succeed. Offer yourself grace in those tough moments, and you'll find that this helps you return to the practice. You will encounter days when you have trouble making time for your practice. Some days your meditation session may feel clunky and awkward. Don't give up. Start fresh the next day. Be gentle with yourself. Above all, embrace the beauty of being a beginner.

Chapter Five

PRACTICE, NOT PERFECTION

One cannot begin to face the real difficulties of the life of prayer and meditation unless one is first perfectly content to be a beginner and really experience [oneself] as one who knows little or nothing, and has a desperate need to learn.

—Thomas Merton

Our soul waits for the LORD;
[God] is our help and shield.
Our heart is glad in [God],
because we trust in [God's] holy name.
Let your steadfast love, O LORD, be upon us,
even as we hope in you.

—Psalm 33:20-22

One of my dearest friends has a prestigious doctoral degree from an exclusive school. When she encounters a roadblock—spiritual or otherwise—she does what she calls "getting smart." She arms herself with knowledge, reading all she can about the topic to shore herself up for the practice that is yet to come. This is what we've done in chapters one through four. We've begun with the *what* and *why* and *how* of meditation. We've outlined scripture, history, theology, and early Christianity's relationship with contemplative practices, as well as the evidence-based scientific benefits of meditation. Though our prayer lives are robust, we understand the distinction between holding space for conversation with God (prayer) and holding space for quiet attentiveness to encounter God's presence (meditation). In meditation, we do more *listening* for God—being still in order to feel God's movement.

We've gotten smart; now it's time to dive in.

BREATH MEDITATION

Our first meditation method (and the first eight days of our practice) is breath meditation. Breath meditation is the go-to meditation tool for beginners for a few reasons. First, our breath is always with us, which means we can practice breath meditation anywhere and anytime. Second, it's the foundation for other meditation techniques. We will rely on our knowledge and experience of breath meditation in order to practice the other four methods in this book.

In Job, we read, "The spirit of God has made me, and the breath of the Almighty gives me life" (33:4). The psalmist writes, "By the word of the LORD the heavens were made, and all their host by the breath of [God's] mouth" (Ps. 33:6). Everything in creation has been made by God and has been given life by the breath of God—including humans. (See Genesis 2:7.) Our breath—our life source—is God within us, all day, every day. But we don't think about our breath until something goes wrong and we cannot breathe or have trouble breathing. Becoming aware of this life force—which comes from God—is the first step in any meditation practice. Slowing, deepening, and smoothing our breathing helps us notice this God-given gift of air.

Though seemingly simple (it's just breathing after all), breath meditation can be challenging. Here are the steps:

1. Sit comfortably in a chair, on the floor, or on a cushion. If you need to stand because of pain or limb stiffness, that's OK. Sitting, however, is the preferred posture because of its ability to deepen relaxation and lower blood pressure and pulse. If you must stand, ensure that you can maintain your balance if you choose to close your eyes. Sit (or stand) tall, allowing your shoulders to sink away from your ears. Ground your sit bones into the chair, cushion, or floor. Rest your palms on your thighs. If you are sleepy, turn your palms up toward the sky; otherwise, palms down.

2. Begin breathing deeply and slowly. I invite you to close your eyes and focus *only* on your breath. Inhale through your nose, and exhale through your mouth. Become aware of each inhalation and exhalation. Is each breath light or heavy? deep or shallow? slow or fast? smooth or staccato?

3. As you continue to be aware of your breath, try to breathe deeply, slowly, and smoothly. If you find counting to be helpful to measure each deep breath, count to four with each inhalation and exhalation. But be careful not to hold your breath; simply practice taking purposeful breaths. If you feel comfortable, place your hands on your stomach and try "belly breathing," engaging the diaphragm and "filling" the belly with air as the rib cage widens. As you exhale through your mouth, allow your belly to relax.

4. Continue breathing deeply, slowly, and smoothly. Notice how you feel. Aim to make the texture of your breathing as even as possible. As you inhale, imagine God's light and love filling your body—from the crown of your head to your toes. As you exhale, imagine letting go of all that is not God—fear, stress, anxiety, pride, ego, anger, bitterness, and resentment. Continue this process, imagining yourself bathed in and illuminated by God's light and love.

5. When your mind wanders or distraction comes knocking, don't jump to judgment or annoyance. Gently return your focus to your breath. A wandering or distracted mind is completely natural. If this happens once, ten times, 100 times, or 10,000 times, imagine it as an opportunity—not a problem—to invite yourself back to your breath and to God.

6. Continue your deep, slow, smooth breathing until the three minutes are up. Inhale God's light; exhale stress.

7. When you have practiced for three minutes, slowly open your eyes and bring yourself back to awareness through gentle movements in your body. Wiggle your toes, roll your shoulders back and down, or stretch if you need to. Then, record what happened in the Daily Examen section.

Day One

BREATH MEDITATION

FREEDOM STATEMENT

Today, I begin my journey drawing nearer to the Divine. I release all judgment and acknowledge that the spiritual life is a practice—not an exercise in perfection.

OPENING

Be still, and know that I am God. | Be still and know. | Be still. | Be.

PRACTICE

Engage in three minutes of breath meditation. Become aware of your breath with each inhalation and exhalation. Breathe slowly and deeply until your breathing becomes smooth. When you feel distracted, gently return your attention to your breath.

CLOSING

Be. | Be still. | Be still and know. | Be still, and know that I am God.

DAILY EXAMEN

God with Us. How did you feel God's presence during this daily meditation, if at all?

Gratitude. Offer thanks to God for giving you the breath of life. Give thanks for the ways in which you felt God's presence before, during, and after your meditation.

Growth. What challenged you today? What came easily today?

Hope. What do you hope tomorrow's meditation practice will bring?

Day Two

BREATH MEDITATION

FREEDOM STATEMENT

Amid the chaos and anxiety of life, breathing can be difficult. As I explore the invitation to connect with my breath—my life source—I will be gentle with myself. I will remind myself to breathe deeply, slowly, and smoothly. I will focus on progress, not perfection.

OPENING

Be still, and know that I am God. | Be still and know. | Be still. | Be.

PRACTICE

Engage in three minutes of breath meditation. Become aware of your breath with each inhalation and exhalation. Breathe slowly and deeply until your breathing becomes smooth. When you feel distracted, gently return your attention to your breath.

CLOSING

Be. | Be still. | Be still and know. | Be still, and know that I am God.

DAILY EXAMEN

God with Us. How did you feel God's presence during this daily meditation, if at all?

Gratitude. Offer thanks to God for giving you the breath of life. Give thanks for the ways in which you felt God's presence before, during, and after your meditation.

Growth. What challenged you today? What came easily today?

Hope. What do you hope tomorrow's meditation practice will bring?

Day Three

BREATH MEDITATION

FREEDOM STATEMENT
Today, I take another step on the journey of connecting with the life force within me. Thoughts will come and go; my mind will wander. Even so, I have but one thing to do for the next three minutes: just breathe.

OPENING
Be still, and know that I am God. | Be still and know. | Be still. | Be.

PRACTICE
Engage in three minutes of breath meditation. Become aware of your breath with each inhalation and exhalation. Breathe slowly and deeply until your breathing becomes smooth. When you feel distracted, gently return your attention to your breath.

CLOSING
Be. | Be still. | Be still and know. | Be still, and know that I am God.

DAILY EXAMEN
God with Us. How did you feel God's presence during this daily meditation, if at all?

Gratitude. Offer thanks to God for giving you the breath of life. Give thanks for the ways in which you felt God's presence before, during, and after your meditation.

Growth. What challenged you today? What came easily today?

Hope. What do you hope tomorrow's meditation practice will bring?

Day Four

BREATH MEDITATION

FREEDOM STATEMENT

Though it is inside me, my breath—God within me—can be difficult to harness. But my practice is beginning to make it possible. Simply noticing my breath for three minutes at a time is more than I was doing four days ago. I continue to commit to this practice and give God thanks for my life force. I'm proud of myself for taking the time to turn inward.

OPENING

Be still, and know that I am God. | Be still and know. | Be still. | Be.

PRACTICE

Engage in three minutes of breath meditation. Become aware of your breath with each inhalation and exhalation. Breathe slowly and deeply until your breathing becomes smooth. When you feel distracted, gently return your attention to your breath.

CLOSING

Be. | Be still. | Be still and know. | Be still, and know that I am God.

DAILY EXAMEN

God with Us. How did you feel God's presence during this daily meditation, if at all?

Gratitude. Offer thanks to God for giving you the breath of life. Give thanks for the ways in which you felt God's presence before, during, and after your meditation.

Growth. What challenged you today? What came easily today?

Hope. What do you hope tomorrow's meditation practice will bring?

BREATH MEDITATION

FREEDOM STATEMENT

How quickly I take for granted the air that God has given me. If I become frustrated, may I be reminded of the gift that is my breath. In moments when I want to quit, may I remember to practice gratitude for the present, one breath at a time.

OPENING

Be still, and know that I am God. | Be still and know. | Be still. | Be.

PRACTICE

Engage in three minutes of breath meditation. Become aware of your breath with each inhalation and exhalation. Breathe slowly and deeply until your breathing becomes smooth. When you feel distracted, gently return your attention to your breath.

CLOSING

Be. | Be still. | Be still and know. | Be still, and know that I am God.

DAILY EXAMEN

God with Us. How did you feel God's presence during this daily meditation, if at all?

Gratitude. Offer thanks to God for giving you the breath of life. Give thanks for the ways in which you felt God's presence before, during, and after your meditation.

Growth. What challenged you today? What came easily today?

Hope. What do you hope tomorrow's meditation practice will bring?

Day Six

BREATH MEDITATION

FREEDOM STATEMENT

Today, I choose to acknowledge the presence of breath within me, every minute and every hour. As I deepen, slow, and smooth my breath, may I be reminded that every breath is a gift.

OPENING

Be still, and know that I am God. | Be still and know. | Be still. | Be.

PRACTICE

Engage in three minutes of breath meditation. Become aware of your breath with each inhalation and exhalation. Breathe slowly and deeply until your breathing becomes smooth. When you feel distracted, gently return your attention to your breath.

CLOSING

Be. | Be still. | Be still and know. | Be still, and know that I am God.

DAILY EXAMEN

God with Us. How did you feel God's presence during this daily meditation, if at all?

Gratitude. Offer thanks to God for giving you the breath of life. Give thanks for the ways in which you felt God's presence before, during, and after your meditation.

Growth. What challenged you today? What came easily today?

Hope. What do you hope tomorrow's meditation practice will bring?

Day Seven

BREATH MEDITATION

FREEDOM STATEMENT
God has gifted me with every breath I take. May I never fail to recognize this gift.

OPENING
Be still, and know that I am God. | Be still and know. | Be still. | Be.

PRACTICE
Engage in three minutes of breath meditation. Become aware of your breath with each inhalation and exhalation. Breathe slowly and deeply until your breathing becomes smooth. When you feel distracted, gently return your attention to your breath.

CLOSING
Be. | Be still. | Be still and know. | Be still, and know that I am God.

DAILY EXAMEN
God with Us. How did you feel God's presence during this daily meditation, if at all?

Gratitude. Offer thanks to God for giving you the breath of life. Give thanks for the ways in which you felt God's presence before, during, and after your meditation.

Growth. What challenged you today? What came easily today?

Hope. What do you hope tomorrow's meditation practice will bring?

Day Eight

BREATH MEDITATION

FREEDOM STATEMENT

Today, I complete my first eight days of drawing nearer to God through my breath. Amid challenges, joy, struggles, and hope, I began this journey. May I continue to be grateful for the time I took to pause, breathe, and notice God's presence within and around me.

OPENING

Be still, and know that I am God. | Be still and know. | Be still. | Be.

PRACTICE

Engage in three minutes of breath meditation. Become aware of your breath with each inhalation and exhalation. Breathe slowly and deeply until your breathing becomes smooth. When you feel distracted, gently return your attention to your breath.

CLOSING

Be. | Be still. | Be still and know. | Be still, and know that I am God.

DAILY EXAMEN

God with Us. How did you feel God's presence during this daily meditation, if at all?

Gratitude. Offer thanks to God for giving you the breath of life. Give thanks for the ways in which you felt God's presence before, during, and after your meditation.

Growth. What challenged you today? What came easily today?

Hope. What do you hope tomorrow's meditation practice will bring?

CENTERING MEDITATION

Next to breath meditation, centering meditation is one of the more readily accessible meditation methods. This form of meditation is inspired by and derived from Centering Prayer, but they are not identical. For centering meditation, we will use our breath and our mind to invite, open, and hold space for God's presence through a sacred word. This word arrives from the Spirit, and we may even find that it changes mid-meditation, especially if we forcefully assigned ourselves a word instead of waiting for the word God invites us to. May we open our mind, heart, hands, and soul to the word God intends for us. May we allow it to surprise and challenge us. When our minds become cluttered with thoughts and ideas, centering meditation—like breath meditation—keeps us focused on an intention: being still and quiet in order to turn inward and connect with God and ourselves.

1. Assume a posture of stillness and quiet—much like you did for breath meditation. In your quiet time and place, be still. Center yourself with at least six deep breaths, using the steps from breath meditation. Notice your inhale and exhale as you breathe deeply, slowly, and smoothly.

2. Ask God for a word or phrase, and listen for it in the stillness. Once you have slowed your breath and focused your mind, invite God to speak to you through a word or phrase. Listen intently for it. Open yourself to what the Spirit has in mind. Release the temptation to control this word. The Spirit will send you the word you need today, even if it feels "off" or not what you wanted. Trust the triune God. Your word might be *anything*. Don't be surprised if it is something you never imagined you would use in meditation. Allow the Spirit to work in mysterious ways. If a word doesn't immediately arrive, don't fret. Simply continue with your breathing, and remain open to any possibility.

3. When your word or phrase arrives, sit with it and hold it in your mind's eye. I like to visualize my word or phrase and repeat it silently with every inhale and exhale. Focus on your word or phrase and continue to breathe purposefully. When and if you become distracted, gently return to your word, just as you returned to your breath. Grace yourself; there is no judgment in meditation practice, only growth and hope. Be open to what God might be inviting you to or telling you through that word. When your session is complete, write about your word in your Daily Examen.[1]

Day Nine

CENTERING MEDITATION

FREEDOM STATEMENT

Today, I release my own agenda. I open myself up to the Holy Spirit and God's invitation to me through a sacred word or phrase. When it comes, I'll hold it—even if it's challenging—for Jacob taught me that wrestling always yields a blessing.

OPENING

Be still, and know that I am God. | Be still and know. | Be still. | Be.

PRACTICE

Engage in three minutes of centering meditation. Beginning with breath meditation as your foundation, find a deep and smooth breathing pattern. Ask God to send you a word or phrase, then listen. When you receive your centering word or phrase, hold it in your mind's eye. Repeat it over and over to harness your focus and consider its invitation. Rest in your word.

CLOSING

Be. | Be still. | Be still and know. | Be still, and know that I am God.

DAILY EXAMEN

God with Us. How did you feel God's presence during this daily meditation, if at all?

Gratitude. Offer thanks to God for giving you the breath of life. Give thanks for the ways in which you felt God's presence before, during, and after your meditation.

Growth. What challenged you today? What came easily today?

Hope. What do you hope tomorrow's meditation practice will bring?

Day Ten

CENTERING MEDITATION

FREEDOM STATEMENT
Listening for God is no easy task. But I have faith that God will meet me where I am. I have faith that God will send me what I need, when I need it.

OPENING
Be still, and know that I am God. | Be still and know. | Be still. | Be.

PRACTICE
Engage in three minutes of centering meditation. Beginning with breath meditation as your foundation, find a deep and smooth breathing pattern. Ask God to send you a word or phrase, then listen. When you receive your centering word or phrase, hold it in your mind's eye. Repeat it over and over to harness your focus and consider its invitation. Rest in your word.

CLOSING
Be. | Be still. | Be still and know. | Be still, and know that I am God.

DAILY EXAMEN
God with Us. How did you feel God's presence during this daily meditation, if at all?

Gratitude. Offer thanks to God for giving you the breath of life. Give thanks for the ways in which you felt God's presence before, during, and after your meditation.

Growth. What challenged you today? What came easily today?

Hope. What do you hope tomorrow's meditation practice will bring?

Day Eleven

CENTERING MEDITATION

FREEDOM STATEMENT
God has much to share with me if only I take the time to listen.

OPENING
Be still, and know that I am God. | Be still and know. | Be still. | Be.

PRACTICE
Engage in three minutes of centering meditation. Beginning with breath meditation as your foundation, find a deep and smooth breathing pattern. Ask God to send you a word or phrase, then listen. When you receive your centering word or phrase, hold it in your mind's eye. Repeat it over and over to harness your focus and consider its invitation. Rest in your word.

CLOSING
Be. | Be still. | Be still and know. | Be still, and know that I am God.

DAILY EXAMEN
God with Us. How did you feel God's presence during this daily meditation, if at all?

Gratitude. Offer thanks to God for giving you the breath of life. Give thanks for the ways in which you felt God's presence before, during, and after your meditation.

Growth. What challenged you today? What came easily today?

Hope. What do you hope tomorrow's meditation practice will bring?

Day Twelve

CENTERING MEDITATION

FREEDOM STATEMENT

Opening my heart to receive a word or phrase from God can be scary. May I listen intently, leaving behind my fear, ego, will, and agenda so that I may consider the invitation God has for me.

OPENING

Be still, and know that I am God. | Be still and know. | Be still. | Be.

PRACTICE

Engage in three minutes of centering meditation. Beginning with breath meditation as your foundation, find a deep and smooth breathing pattern. Ask God to send you a word or phrase, then listen. When you receive your centering word or phrase, hold it in your mind's eye. Repeat it over and over to harness your focus and consider its invitation. Rest in your word.

CLOSING

Be. | Be still. | Be still and know. | Be still, and know that I am God.

DAILY EXAMEN

God with Us. How did you feel God's presence during this daily meditation, if at all?

Gratitude. Offer thanks to God for giving you the breath of life. Give thanks for the ways in which you felt God's presence before, during, and after your meditation.

Growth. What challenged you today? What came easily today?

Hope. What do you hope tomorrow's meditation practice will bring?

Day Thirteen

CENTERING MEDITATION

FREEDOM STATEMENT
Patiently listening for God is no easy task. But I have faith that God will care for me as I seek God's wisdom.

OPENING
Be still, and know that I am God. | Be still and know. | Be still. | Be.

PRACTICE
Engage in three minutes of centering meditation. Beginning with breath meditation as your foundation, find a deep and smooth breathing pattern. Ask God to send you a word or phrase, then listen. When you receive your centering word or phrase, hold it in your mind's eye. Repeat it over and over to harness your focus and consider its invitation. Rest in your word.

CLOSING
Be. | Be still. | Be still and know. | Be still, and know that I am God.

DAILY EXAMEN
God with Us. How did you feel God's presence during this daily meditation, if at all?

Gratitude. Offer thanks to God for giving you the breath of life. Give thanks for the ways in which you felt God's presence before, during, and after your meditation.

Growth. What challenged you today? What came easily today?

Hope. What do you hope tomorrow's meditation practice will bring?

Day Fourteen

CENTERING MEDITATION

FREEDOM STATEMENT

The more I practice meditation, the more I yearn for this time to sit still and listen. Even when I feel tired, restless, and vulnerable, I know that listening for God's still small voice helps me receive the peace that passes all understanding.

OPENING

Be still, and know that I am God. | Be still and know. | Be still. | Be.

PRACTICE

Engage in three minutes of centering meditation. Beginning with breath meditation as your foundation, find a deep and smooth breathing pattern. Ask God to send you a word or phrase, then listen. When you receive your centering word or phrase, hold it in your mind's eye. Repeat it over and over to harness your focus and consider its invitation. Rest in your word.

CLOSING

Be. | Be still. | Be still and know. | Be still, and know that I am God.

DAILY EXAMEN

God with Us. How did you feel God's presence during this daily meditation, if at all?

Gratitude. Offer thanks to God for giving you the breath of life. Give thanks for the ways in which you felt God's presence before, during, and after your meditation.

Growth. What challenged you today? What came easily today?

Hope. What do you hope tomorrow's meditation practice will bring?

Day Fifteen

CENTERING MEDITATION

Freedom Statement

During this practice, many words have come to my heart and mind—words that I didn't know I needed to hear and consider. May I continue to be open to receiving God's wisdom for me, even when it's difficult to accept.

Opening

Be still, and know that I am God. | Be still and know. | Be still. | Be.

Practice

Engage in three minutes of centering meditation. Beginning with breath meditation as your foundation, find a deep and smooth breathing pattern. Ask God to send you a word or phrase, then listen. When you receive your centering word or phrase, hold it in your mind's eye. Repeat it over and over to harness your focus and consider its invitation. Rest in your word.

Closing

Be. | Be still. | Be still and know. | Be still, and know that I am God.

Daily Examen

God with Us. How did you feel God's presence during this daily meditation, if at all?

Gratitude. Offer thanks to God for giving you the breath of life. Give thanks for the ways in which you felt God's presence before, during, and after your meditation.

Growth. What challenged you today? What came easily today?

Hope. What do you hope tomorrow's meditation practice will bring?

Day Sixteen

CENTERING MEDITATION

FREEDOM STATEMENT

During this practice, I have opened my heart and soul to God's invitation to me through a sacred word or phrase. I have held to God's wisdom—even when it was challenging. I have wrestled, and, indeed, I was blessed.

OPENING

Be still, and know that I am God. | Be still and know. | Be still. | Be.

PRACTICE

Engage in three minutes of centering meditation. Beginning with breath meditation as your foundation, find a deep and smooth breathing pattern. Ask God to send you a word or phrase, then listen. When you receive your centering word or phrase, hold it in your mind's eye. Repeat it over and over to harness your focus and consider its invitation. Rest in your word.

CLOSING

Be. | Be still. | Be still and know. | Be still, and know that I am God.

DAILY EXAMEN

God with Us. How did you feel God's presence during this daily meditation, if at all?

Gratitude. Offer thanks to God for giving you the breath of life. Give thanks for the ways in which you felt God's presence before, during, and after your meditation.

Growth. What challenged you today? What came easily today?

Hope. What do you hope tomorrow's meditation practice will bring?

LECTIO DIVINA MEDITATION

Lectio divina is Latin for "sacred reading" or "divine reading." *Lectio divina* is a specific process of using our beginner's mind (not our analytical or exegetical cognitive skills) to examine scripture in a new light. To practice *lectio divina*, we listen to a text read aloud slowly and deliberately several times and pay attention to a word or phrase within the text that "shimmers" for us. Historically, the practice contains four parts: *lectio* ("to read"), *meditatio* ("to reflect"), *oratio* ("to respond"), and *comtemplatio* ("to rest").[2]

In this book, a scripture passage accompanies each day's practice. You may read it aloud for yourself, or, if in a group, have someone else read it aloud. These passages are short and meant to be read several times. Like centering meditation, *lectio divina* focuses on a word or phrase. The practices differ, however, in that scripture directly inspires the word or phrase in *lectio divina*.

Use the following steps when practicing *lectio divina* meditation:

1. **Open.** Read the Freedom Statement and complete the Opening ritual. Center yourself with breath meditation until you are in a state of quiet, slow, smooth, and deep breathing.

2. **Read/*Lectio*.** Read the scripture aloud slowly with your beginner's mind; do not analyze or exegete the passage. Simply read or listen. Find a word that stands out to you, invites you, speaks to you, calls to you, or challenges you. Hold that word in your heart and mind.

3. **Reflect/*Meditatio*.** Read the scripture aloud again, slowly and deliberately. Did the same word or phrase stand out? Relish it. Sit with it. Allow the Holy Spirit to pull you into the presence of God using that word. Ask yourself, *What is this word inviting me to today? How might God be calling out to me through this piece of scripture?* Repeat your word or phrase silently to yourself.

4. **Respond/*Oratio*.** Respond to the word given to you. What questions do you have about the word or phrase? What does this word mean to you today? Be open to listening and receiving God's response. Know that God doesn't always speak loudly; listen for the still small voice, a whisper, a feeling, or an awareness. Tell God what you heard or felt.

5. **Rest/*Contemplatio*.** Rest with your word or phrase and what you heard. Give thanks for the word and what you learned.[3, 4]

LECTIO DIVINA MEDITATION

FREEDOM STATEMENT
Today, I seek God's wisdom through God's holy scripture. I trust that God will show me what I need to glean and invite me to dig deeper. May I be open to receiving a sacred word from God.

OPENING
Be still, and know that I am God. | Be still and know. | Be still. | Be.

PRACTICE
Once your breathing is slow, smooth, and deep, engage in three minutes of *lectio divina* meditation. Read today's scripture passage (printed below) several times. Consider what word within the text is "shimmering" for you. Reflect on that word. What does it mean to you today? What might be God's invitation to you through this word? Finally, rest in your word.

READ ISAIAH 55:8-9.
For my thoughts are not your thoughts,
    nor are your ways my ways, says the LORD.
For as the heavens are higher than the earth,
    so are my ways higher than your ways
    and my thoughts than your thoughts.

CLOSING
Be. | Be still. | Be still and know. | Be still, and know that I am God.

DAILY EXAMEN
God with Us. How did you feel God's presence during this daily meditation, if at all?

Gratitude. Offer thanks to God for giving you the breath of life. Give thanks for the ways in which you felt God's presence before, during, and after your meditation.

Growth. What challenged you today? What came easily today?

Hope. What do you hope tomorrow's meditation practice will bring?

LECTIO DIVINA MEDITATION

FREEDOM STATEMENT

I have much to learn through scripture. May I be open to receiving, reflecting upon, responding to, and resting in God's Word.

OPENING

Be still, and know that I am God. | Be still and know. | Be still. | Be.

PRACTICE

Once your breathing is slow, smooth, and deep, engage in three minutes of *lectio divina* meditation. Read today's scripture passage (printed below) several times. Consider what word within the text is "shimmering" for you. Reflect on that word. What does it mean to you today? What might be God's invitation to you through this word? Finally, rest in your word.

READ PSALM 23:1-3.

The LORD is my shepherd, I shall not want.
    He makes me lie down in green pastures;
he leads me beside still waters;
    he restores my soul.
He leads me in right paths
    for his name's sake.

CLOSING

Be. | Be still. | Be still and know. | Be still, and know that I am God.

DAILY EXAMEN

God with Us. How did you feel God's presence during this daily meditation, if at all?

Gratitude. Offer thanks to God for giving you the breath of life. Give thanks for the ways in which you felt God's presence before, during, and after your meditation.

Growth. What challenged you today? What came easily today?

Hope. What do you hope tomorrow's meditation practice will bring?

Day Nineteen

LECTIO DIVINA MEDITATION

FREEDOM STATEMENT
Scripture is the path through which I can reconnect with God and discover all that I am called to do. May I embrace this time as a sacred invitation into God's presence.

OPENING
Be still, and know that I am God. | Be still and know. | Be still. | Be.

PRACTICE
Once your breathing is slow, smooth, and deep, engage in three minutes of *lectio divina* meditation. Read today's scripture passage (printed below) several times. Consider what word within the text is "shimmering" for you. Reflect on that word. What does it mean to you today? What might be God's invitation to you through this word? Finally, rest in your word.

READ PSALM 25:4-5 (NIV).
Show me your ways, LORD,
 teach me your paths.
Guide me in your truth and teach me,
 for you are God my Savior,
 and my hope is in you all day long.

CLOSING
Be. | Be still. | Be still and know. | Be still, and know that I am God.

DAILY EXAMEN
God with Us. How did you feel God's presence during this daily meditation, if at all?

Gratitude. Offer thanks to God for giving you the breath of life. Give thanks for the ways in which you felt God's presence before, during, and after your meditation.

Growth. What challenged you today? What came easily today?

Hope. What do you hope tomorrow's meditation practice will bring?

LECTIO DIVINA MEDITATION

FREEDOM STATEMENT
Scripture is not always easy. It pushes and challenges me, even as it frees me and fills me. May I grace myself and continue to be open to learning more about myself and God through this sacred text.

OPENING
Be still, and know that I am God. | Be still and know. | Be still. | Be.

PRACTICE
Once your breathing is slow, smooth, and deep, engage in three minutes of *lectio divina* meditation. Read today's scripture passage (printed below) several times. Consider what word within the text is "shimmering" for you. Reflect on that word. What does it mean to you today? What might be God's invitation to you through this word? Finally, rest in your word.

READ PSALM 63:1.
O God, you are my God, I seek you,
    my soul thirsts for you;
my flesh faints for you,
    as in a dry and weary land where there is no water.

CLOSING
Be. | Be still. | Be still and know. | Be still, and know that I am God.

DAILY EXAMEN
God with Us. How did you feel God's presence during this daily meditation, if at all?

Gratitude. Offer thanks to God for giving you the breath of life. Give thanks for the ways in which you felt God's presence before, during, and after your meditation.

Growth. What challenged you today? What came easily today?

Hope. What do you hope tomorrow's meditation practice will bring?

Day Twenty-One

LECTIO DIVINA MEDITATION

FREEDOM STATEMENT

With each day and each text, I learn something new about myself and God. Even as I wrestle to find my blessing, may I continue to move along this path of spiritual progress—not perfection.

OPENING

Be still, and know that I am God. | Be still and know. | Be still. | Be.

PRACTICE

Once your breathing is slow, smooth, and deep, engage in three minutes of *lectio divina* meditation. Read today's scripture passage (printed below) several times. Consider what word within the text is "shimmering" for you. Reflect on that word. What does it mean to you today? What might be God's invitation to you through this word? Finally, rest in your word.

READ ISAIAH 40:31 (KJV).

They that wait upon the LORD shall renew their strength; they shall mount up with wings as eagles; they shall run, and not be weary; and they shall walk, and not faint.

CLOSING

Be. | Be still. | Be still and know. | Be still, and know that I am God.

DAILY EXAMEN

God with Us. How did you feel God's presence during this daily meditation, if at all?

Gratitude. Offer thanks to God for giving you the breath of life. Give thanks for the ways in which you felt God's presence before, during, and after your meditation.

Growth. What challenged you today? What came easily today?

Hope. What do you hope tomorrow's meditation practice will bring?

LECTIO DIVINA MEDITATION

FREEDOM STATEMENT
May I glean from God's Word the lessons that I need most today. May I be open to the Holy Spirit's movement in this text, as well as the movement within my heart.

OPENING
Be still, and know that I am God. | Be still and know. | Be still. | Be.

PRACTICE
Once your breathing is slow, smooth, and deep, engage in three minutes of *lectio divina* meditation. Read today's scripture passage (printed below) several times. Consider what word within the text is "shimmering" for you. Reflect on that word. What does it mean to you today? What might be God's invitation to you through this word? Finally, rest in your word.

READ ISAIAH 60:1 (KJV).
Arise, shine; for thy light is come, and the glory of the LORD is risen upon thee.

CLOSING
Be. | Be still. | Be still and know. | Be still, and know that I am God.

DAILY EXAMEN
God with Us. How did you feel God's presence during this daily meditation, if at all?

Gratitude. Offer thanks to God for giving you the breath of life. Give thanks for the ways in which you felt God's presence before, during, and after your meditation.

Growth. What challenged you today? What came easily today?

Hope. What do you hope tomorrow's meditation practice will bring?

Day Twenty-Three

LECTIO DIVINA MEDITATION

FREEDOM STATEMENT

Each day, something emerges from my engagement with these texts. Sometimes it's small; other days, it's large and overwhelming. May I learn to take this practice one day at a time and to trust God to reveal exactly what I need to hear, when I need to hear it.

OPENING

Be still, and know that I am God. | Be still and know. | Be still. | Be.

PRACTICE

Once your breathing is slow, smooth, and deep, engage in three minutes of *lectio divina* meditation. Read today's scripture passage (printed below) several times. Consider what word within the text is "shimmering" for you. Reflect on that word. What does it mean to you today? What might be God's invitation to you through this word? Finally, rest in your word.

READ JEREMIAH 29:11-13.

Surely I know the plans I have for you, says the LORD, plans for your welfare and not for harm, to give you a future with hope. Then when you call upon me and come and pray to me, I will hear you. When you search for me, you will find me; if you seek me with all your heart.

CLOSING

Be. | Be still. | Be still and know. | Be still, and know that I am God.

DAILY EXAMEN

God with Us. How did you feel God's presence during this daily meditation, if at all?

Gratitude. Offer thanks to God for giving you the breath of life. Give thanks for the ways in which you felt God's presence before, during, and after your meditation.

Growth. What challenged you today? What came easily today?

Hope. What do you hope tomorrow's meditation practice will bring?

Day Twenty-Four

LECTIO DIVINA MEDITATION

FREEDOM STATEMENT
I have learned much through the process of *lectio divina*. May I continue to be open to receiving, reflecting on, responding to, and resting in God's Word.

OPENING
Be still, and know that I am God. | Be still and know. | Be still. | Be.

PRACTICE
Once your breathing is slow, smooth, and deep, engage in three minutes of *lectio divina* meditation. Read today's scripture passage (printed below) several times. Consider what word within the text is "shimmering" for you. Reflect on that word. What does it mean to you today? What might be God's invitation to you through this word? Finally, rest in your word.

READ GALATIANS 5:22-23.
The fruit of the Spirit is love, joy, peace, patience, kindness, generosity, faithfulness, gentleness, and self-control. There is no law against such things.

CLOSING
Be. | Be still. | Be still and know. | Be still, and know that I am God.

DAILY EXAMEN
God with Us. How did you feel God's presence during this daily meditation, if at all?

Gratitude. Offer thanks to God for giving you the breath of life. Give thanks for the ways in which you felt God's presence before, during, and after your meditation.

Growth. What challenged you today? What came easily today?

Hope. What do you hope tomorrow's meditation practice will bring?

LOVING-KINDNESS MEDITATION

Humans are notorious for being less than gentle with themselves and others. We live in a culture that is hypercritical about appearances, productivity, failure, relationships, and success. Extending love to ourselves and others may not be the easiest thing to do. Loving-kindness meditation originates from a Buddhist practice, but Jesus teaches the same ideal in the Gospels: "'Love the Lord your God with all your heart, and with all your soul, and with all your mind.' . . . 'Love your neighbor as yourself'" (Matt. 22:37, 39). Love and kindness, therefore, reside at the heart of Christianity. But how do we love ourselves and each other in a world that makes it so difficult to do so? We practice.

Loving-kindness meditation invites us to recognize and accept the love that God extends to us so that we in turn may extend it to others—both to those whom we love and to those who cause us frustration. It also guides us as we learn how to offer love to others until offering it becomes second nature. In this practice, we embody God's love and direct that love toward another person. Loving-kindness meditation is different from praying for someone. How so? Well, let's consider our child, spouse, partner, parent, sibling, or best friend. The love we feel for them is so strong and deep that we feel their pain when they suffer. What we feel for our dear ones is merely a fraction of the infinite and transcendent love God feels for us. Loving-kindness meditation allows us to embody that love and extend it to others.

To begin, start with the foundation of breath meditation. Once in a comfortable breathing pattern that is slow, deep, and smooth, begin the four-step process:

1. As you breathe deeply, slowly, and smoothly, picture yourself in your mind's eye. As you see yourself, imagine God's love and light enveloping you with warmth. Soak in God's love and kindness as if you are wrapping yourself in a soft blanket on a winter evening. How do you feel? As you allow this belovedness to pour over you and move through you, repeat these phrases, embodying the full light and energy from God and directing it toward yourself silently or aloud:

May I be safe.
May I be happy.
May I be healthy.
May I be at peace.

2. Once you are full of God's love, picture a loved one in your mind's eye. Extend that same love and kindness that God gifted to you to your loved one using these phrases:

May [name] be safe.

May [name] be happy.

May [name] be healthy.

May [name] be at peace.

3. Next, picture someone who frustrates, angers, or annoys you. This might be someone you don't care for or someone who has wronged you. It could be someone who needs your forgiveness—or someone from whom you need forgiveness. It could be someone you know well or someone you've never met. Allow that same love and kindness that God poured into you and that you extended to your love one to extend to this person. Push through your animosity, bitterness, or resentment, and practice holding him or her in love and light.

May [name] be safe.

May [name] be happy.

May [name] be healthy.

May [name] be at peace.

4. Finally, extend God's love even further. Picture all God's creation—every human, plant, and animal. Extend loving-kindness to everyone and everything—generously and sincerely, especially to those whom you deem strangers.

May all God's creation be safe.

May all God's creation be happy.

May all God's creation be healthy.

May all God's creation be at peace.[5]

Loving-kindness meditation can be the most powerful of the five tools in this book. In all the sessions that I've taught it, practitioners say it is the most moving for them—but also the most difficult. The loving-kindness practice exemplifies the gospel at its core as it invites us to think about, reflect on, and attend to the essence of our beings—love. And this love implores us to practice what Jesus teaches. He says the most important commandment is to love God and one another. Jesus embodies love, and he expects us to do the same. When we practice loving-kindness meditation—extending it to ourselves, our loved ones, our enemies, and all of creation—we embody a powerful practice that translates into how we behave outside the space of our daily meditation time. Extending God's love to ourselves and all living entities invites us into a posture of awe and respect for God's creation.

LOVING-KINDNESS MEDITATION

FREEDOM STATEMENT
Love is the foundation of everything. Jesus commands me to love God and love my neighbor. He also says, "Love your enemies."

OPENING
Be still, and know that I am God. | Be still and know. | Be still. | Be.

PRACTICE
Once you've settled into your breathing pattern, engage in three minutes of loving-kindness meditation. First, imagine God's love, light, and kindness enveloping you—flowing around and through you. Then, take that same love and extend it to a loved one. Next, extend it to a person whom you dislike. Finally, offer it to all God's creation.

May I/[name] be safe.
May I/[name] be happy.
May I/[name] be healthy.
May I/[name] be at peace.

CLOSING
Be. | Be still. | Be still and know. | Be still, and know that I am God.

DAILY EXAMEN
God with Us. How did you feel God's presence during this daily meditation, if at all?

Gratitude. Offer thanks to God for giving you the breath of life. Give thanks for the ways in which you felt God's presence before, during, and after your meditation.

Growth. What challenged you today? What came easily today?

Hope. What do you hope tomorrow's meditation practice will bring?

Day Twenty-Six

LOVING-KINDNESS MEDITATION

FREEDOM STATEMENT

The triune God values love above all else. But love is hard. May I always remember that I am created for, commanded to, and called to love.

OPENING

Be still, and know that I am God. | Be still and know. | Be still. | Be.

PRACTICE

Once you've settled into your breathing pattern, engage in three minutes of loving-kindness meditation. First, imagine God's love, light, and kindness enveloping you—flowing around and through you. Then, take that same love and extend it to a loved one. Next, extend it to a person whom you dislike. Finally, offer it to all God's creation.

May I/[name] be safe.
May I/[name] be happy.
May I/[name] be healthy.
May I/[name] be at peace.

CLOSING

Be. | Be still. | Be still and know. | Be still, and know that I am God.

DAILY EXAMEN

God with Us. How did you feel God's presence during this daily meditation, if at all?

Gratitude. Offer thanks to God for giving you the breath of life. Give thanks for the ways in which you felt God's presence before, during, and after your meditation.

Growth. What challenged you today? What came easily today?

Hope. What do you hope tomorrow's meditation practice will bring?

Day Twenty-Seven

LOVING-KINDNESS MEDITATION

FREEDOM STATEMENT
Nothing is greater in this world than to love and be loved.

OPENING
Be still, and know that I am God. | Be still and know. | Be still. | Be.

PRACTICE
Once you've settled into your breathing pattern, engage in three minutes of loving-kindness meditation. First, imagine God's love, light, and kindness enveloping you—flowing around and through you. Then, take that same love and extend it to a loved one. Next, extend it to a person whom you dislike. Finally, offer it to all God's creation.

May I/[name] be safe.
May I/[name] be happy.
May I/[name] be healthy.
May I/[name] be at peace.

CLOSING
Be. | Be still. | Be still and know. | Be still, and know that I am God.

DAILY EXAMEN
God with Us. How did you feel God's presence during this daily meditation, if at all?

Gratitude. Offer thanks to God for giving you the breath of life. Give thanks for the ways in which you felt God's presence before, during, and after your meditation.

Growth. What challenged you today? What came easily today?

Hope. What do you hope tomorrow's meditation practice will bring?

LOVING-KINDNESS MEDITATION

FREEDOM STATEMENT

Loving myself and others can be difficult; I don't pretend to get it right every day. Love requires practice.

OPENING

Be still, and know that I am God. | Be still and know. | Be still. | Be.

PRACTICE

Once you've settled into your breathing pattern, engage in three minutes of loving-kindness meditation. First, imagine God's love, light, and kindness enveloping you—flowing around and through you. Then, take that same love and extend it to a loved one. Next, extend it to a person whom you dislike. Finally, offer it to all God's creation.

May I/[name] be safe.
May I/[name] be happy.
May I/[name] be healthy.
May I/[name] be at peace.

CLOSING

Be. | Be still. | Be still and know. | Be still, and know that I am God.

DAILY EXAMEN

God with Us. How did you feel God's presence during this daily meditation, if at all?

Gratitude. Offer thanks to God for giving you the breath of life. Give thanks for the ways in which you felt God's presence before, during, and after your meditation.

Growth. What challenged you today? What came easily today?

Hope. What do you hope tomorrow's meditation practice will bring?

LOVING-KINDNESS MEDITATION

FREEDOM STATEMENT

May I be patient with myself on days when I do not feel like loving myself or others—especially those whom I dislike. May God fill my heart with the desire to love and be kind.

OPENING

Be still, and know that I am God. | Be still and know. | Be still. | Be.

PRACTICE

Once you've settled into your breathing pattern, engage in three minutes of loving-kindness meditation. First, imagine God's love, light, and kindness enveloping you—flowing around and through you. Then, take that same love and extend it to a loved one. Next, extend it to a person whom you dislike. Finally, offer it to all God's creation.

May I/[name] be safe.
May I/[name] be happy.
May I/[name] be healthy.
May I/[name] be at peace.

CLOSING

Be. | Be still. | Be still and know. | Be still, and know that I am God.

DAILY EXAMEN

God with Us. How did you feel God's presence during this daily meditation, if at all?

Gratitude. Offer thanks to God for giving you the breath of life. Give thanks for the ways in which you felt God's presence before, during, and after your meditation.

Growth. What challenged you today? What came easily today?

Hope. What do you hope tomorrow's meditation practice will bring?

LOVING-KINDNESS MEDITATION

FREEDOM STATEMENT
Some days, I can love myself, my friends and family, and my enemies with no difficulty. Other days, it's a constant challenge. On those days, may I practice patience with myself and others.

OPENING
Be still, and know that I am God. | Be still and know. | Be still. | Be.

PRACTICE
Once you've settled into your breathing pattern, engage in three minutes of loving-kindness meditation. First, imagine God's love, light, and kindness enveloping you—flowing around and through you. Then, take that same love and extend it to a loved one. Next, extend it to a person whom you dislike. Finally, offer it to all God's creation.

May I/[name] be safe.
May I/[name] be happy.
May I/[name] be healthy.
May I/[name] be at peace.

CLOSING
Be. | Be still. | Be still and know. | Be still, and know that I am God.

DAILY EXAMEN
God with Us. How did you feel God's presence during this daily meditation, if at all?

Gratitude. Offer thanks to God for giving you the breath of life. Give thanks for the ways in which you felt God's presence before, during, and after your meditation.

Growth. What challenged you today? What came easily today?

Hope. What do you hope tomorrow's meditation practice will bring?

Day Thirty-One

LOVING-KINDNESS MEDITATION

FREEDOM STATEMENT

May I never forget that I am created for love. May I be open to God filling me with love and kindness so that I may extend it to others—no matter how I feel about them.

OPENING

Be still, and know that I am God. | Be still and know. | Be still. | Be.

PRACTICE

Once you've settled into your breathing pattern, engage in three minutes of loving-kindness meditation. First, imagine God's love, light, and kindness enveloping you—flowing around and through you. Then, take that same love and extend it to a loved one. Next, extend it to a person whom you dislike. Finally, offer it to all God's creation.

May I/[name] be safe.
May I/[name] be happy.
May I/[name] be healthy.
May I/[name] be at peace.

CLOSING

Be. | Be still. | Be still and know. | Be still, and know that I am God.

DAILY EXAMEN

God with Us. How did you feel God's presence during this daily meditation, if at all?

Gratitude. Offer thanks to God for giving you the breath of life. Give thanks for the ways in which you felt God's presence before, during, and after your meditation.

Growth. What challenged you today? What came easily today?

Hope. What do you hope tomorrow's meditation practice will bring?

LOVING-KINDNESS MEDITATION

FREEDOM STATEMENT

Love is hard. Love requires sacrifice. When I feel unloved or when I behave unlovingly toward others, may I remember the tremendous love and sacrifice God has extended to me and how I am commanded to extend that love to myself and to others.

OPENING

Be still, and know that I am God. | Be still and know. | Be still. | Be.

PRACTICE

Once you've settled into your breathing pattern, engage in three minutes of loving-kindness meditation. First, imagine God's love, light, and kindness enveloping you—flowing around and through you. Then, take that same love and extend it to a loved one. Next, extend it to a person whom you dislike. Finally, offer it to all God's creation.

May I/[name] be safe.
May I/[name] be happy.
May I/[name] be healthy.
May I/[name] be at peace.

CLOSING

Be. | Be still. | Be still and know. | Be still, and know that I am God.

DAILY EXAMEN

God with Us. How did you feel God's presence during this daily meditation, if at all?

Gratitude. Offer thanks to God for giving you the breath of life. Give thanks for the ways in which you felt God's presence before, during, and after your meditation.

Growth. What challenged you today? What came easily today?

Hope. What do you hope tomorrow's meditation practice will bring?

DEVOTIONAL MEDITATION

There's no shortage of devotion to God in scripture. From Deuteronomy to the Gospels, we are taught to "love the Lord your God with all your heart, and with all your soul, and with all your mind, and with all your strength" (Mark 12:30). But what does it mean to be devoted to and to love God? Does God need our love, affection, time, and attention? Of course!

A devotional meditation practice is one that focuses on God through adoration—love and respect—as well as gratitude, reverence, and veneration. We already practice devotion to God through our worship experiences in our own faith communities. Devotional meditation uses scripture, prayer, mantras, hymns, and Taizé songs to offer humble obeisance to God.

Why do we need a devotional meditation practice? Because most of our thoughts and actions revolve around us. Devotion helps us recalibrate ourselves toward God, who is our rightful Center. It helps us engage in the contemplative practice of *theoria* ("gazing"). When God is our North Star, we can more easily calm our minds and draw nearer to our Creator. In doing so, we become attuned to God's voice and will for our lives. There's no shortage of ways to do this, but here are some examples of devotional meditation.

The Jesus Prayer

This prayer was used by an anonymous Orthodox Christian pilgrim as a way of practicing the ceaseless prayer described in First Thessalonians. The Jesus Prayer is this: "Lord Jesus Christ, Son of God, have mercy on me, a sinner." A shorter version works as well: "Lord Jesus Christ, have mercy on me." This prayer exudes humility. It recognizes Jesus' divinity while also acknowledging our need for mercy and grace. It's not meant to be a derogatory prayer in which we chastise ourselves for sinning. Rather, it acknowledges our humanity while revering Christ's divinity and receiving God's grace.

A Line from a Hymn of Praise or Adoration

- "Be thou my vision, O Lord of my heart." (UMH, no. 451)
- "This is the day that the Lord hath made. Let us rejoice and be glad in it." (UMH, no. 657)

- "O for a thousand tongues to sing my great Redeemer's praise." (UMH, no. 57)
- "Joyful, joyful, [I] adore thee, God of glory, Lord of love." (UMH, no. 89)
- "Praise God, from whom all blessings flow." (UMH, no. 94)
- "Spirit of the living God, fall afresh on me." (UMH, no. 393)

A Line or Verse from a Taizé Song or Contemporary Worship Song

See https://www.taize.fr/en ("At the Wellspring of Faith" section) for a list, as well as the *Upper Room Worshipbook: Music and Liturgies for Spiritual Formation.*

A Favorite Bible Verse

- "The LORD is my Shepherd, I shall not want" (Ps. 23:1).
- "Create in me a clean heart, O God" (Ps. 51:10).
- "O LORD, our Sovereign, how majestic is your name in all the earth!" (Ps. 8:1).
- "Praise the LORD! Praise God in his sanctuary" (Ps. 150:1).
- "Make a joyful noise to the LORD, all the earth" (Ps. 100:1).
- "Praise the LORD, O my soul!" (Ps. 146:1).
- "Taste and see that the LORD is good" (Ps. 34:8).

A Mantra or Prayer

Much like the Jesus Prayer, a mantra is a short sentence or phrase that can be easily memorized and repeated in adoration, devotion, and trust. Create your own, or try one of the following:

- Rejoice in the Lord always.
- I will praise you with all that I am and all that I have.
- God, you are my Rock and my Redeemer.
- Wondrous Lord, I give you thanks and praise this day.
- Lord, make me your servant.

How to Practice Devotional Meditation

Once you have chosen a devotional phrase (or written one of your own), begin with breath meditation. When you have reached a deep, slow, and smooth breathing pattern, introduce your devotional statement. Repeat it to yourself. When you become distracted, simply bring your attention, adoration, and devotion back to worshiping God. Many Christians use visual or tactile objects during devotional meditation to facilitate *theoria*, including rosaries, Protestant prayer beads, a cross, a candle, or an icon of Christ. These are all perfectly appropriate to use in devotional meditation, especially for people prone to fidgeting, mind-wandering, or falling asleep when their eyes are closed.

Don't hinder your practice by thinking these visual and tactile objects are idolatrous. These are merely tools to aid your spirituality; they are what Orthodox Christians call "windows to God." Physical objects are used every Sunday in Christian worship around the world. A church's sanctuary houses many of them: an altar, a candle, a cross, stained-glass windows, colorful banners with Christian symbols, Communion elements, or screens that project song lyrics. Other objects also facilitate our worship: Bibles, hymnals, prayer books, instruments. All these items help the worshiper focus on God.

It is not blasphemy to engage with human-made objects that aid your devotion. In Numbers 15:39, God instructs the Israelites to cling to the tassels on their garments to recall God's commandments: "You have the fringe so that, when you see it, you will remember all the commandments of the LORD and do them, and not follow the lust of your own heart and your own eyes." Early Christian monastics used rocks and strings of beads to help them count the Psalms as they prayed them. You are human and therefore drawn to items that engage your senses. You yearn to see, feel, hear, smell, and taste. Don't create obstacles to your meditation practice by cutting yourself off from these aids.

Day Thirty-Three

DEVOTIONAL MEDITATION

FREEDOM STATEMENT
Showing my devotion to God recalibrates my heart toward its true Center.

OPENING
Be still, and know that I am God. | Be still and know. | Be still. | Be.

PRACTICE
Once you've settled into your breathing pattern, engage in three minutes of devotional meditation. Choose a line from scripture, the Jesus Prayer, a Taizé song, or a hymn or create your own devotional phrase that encapsulates your devotion for and adoration of God. Repeat it to yourself, "gazing" at God in your mind's eye.

CLOSING
Be. | Be still. | Be still and know. | Be still, and know that I am God.

DAILY EXAMEN
God with Us. How did you feel God's presence during this daily meditation, if at all?

Gratitude. Offer thanks to God for giving you the breath of life. Give thanks for the ways in which you felt God's presence before, during, and after your meditation.

Growth. What challenged you today? What came easily today?

Hope. What do you hope tomorrow's meditation practice will bring?

Day Thirty-Four

DEVOTIONAL MEDITATION

FREEDOM STATEMENT
God longs for my devotion. God wants my time, attention, and adoration. God yearns to be in relationship with me, just as I yearn for God.

OPENING
Be still, and know that I am God. | Be still and know. | Be still. | Be.

PRACTICE
Once you've settled into your breathing pattern, engage in three minutes of devotional meditation. Choose a line from scripture, the Jesus Prayer, a Taizé song, or a hymn or create your own devotional phrase that encapsulates your devotion for and adoration of God. Repeat it to yourself, "gazing" at God in your mind's eye.

CLOSING
Be. | Be still. | Be still and know. | Be still, and know that I am God.

DAILY EXAMEN
God with Us. How did you feel God's presence during this daily meditation, if at all?

Gratitude. Offer thanks to God for giving you the breath of life. Give thanks for the ways in which you felt God's presence before, during, and after your meditation.

Growth. What challenged you today? What came easily today?

Hope. What do you hope tomorrow's meditation practice will bring?

Day Thirty-Five

DEVOTIONAL MEDITATION

FREEDOM STATEMENT
May I release anything and everything that inhibits me from lifting my praise and worship to God.

OPENING
Be still, and know that I am God. | Be still and know. | Be still. | Be.

PRACTICE
Once you've settled into your breathing pattern, engage in three minutes of devotional meditation. Choose a line from scripture, the Jesus Prayer, a Taizé song, or a hymn or create your own devotional phrase that encapsulates your devotion for and adoration of God. Repeat it to yourself, "gazing" at God in your mind's eye.

CLOSING
Be. | Be still. | Be still and know. | Be still, and know that I am God.

DAILY EXAMEN
God with Us. How did you feel God's presence during this daily meditation, if at all?

Gratitude. Offer thanks to God for giving you the breath of life. Give thanks for the ways in which you felt God's presence before, during, and after your meditation.

Growth. What challenged you today? What came easily today?

Hope. What do you hope tomorrow's meditation practice will bring?

DEVOTIONAL MEDITATION

FREEDOM STATEMENT

Devotion asks me to practice humility, but so often I believe I am the center of the universe. May I learn humility and trust. I am neither the Maker nor the Maintainer of creation. May I praise the One who is.

OPENING

Be still, and know that I am God. | Be still and know. | Be still. | Be.

PRACTICE

Once you've settled into your breathing pattern, engage in three minutes of devotional meditation. Choose a line from scripture, the Jesus Prayer, a Taizé song, or a hymn or create your own devotional phrase that encapsulates your devotion for and adoration of God. Repeat it to yourself, "gazing" at God in your mind's eye.

CLOSING

Be. | Be still. | Be still and know. | Be still, and know that I am God.

DAILY EXAMEN

God with Us. How did you feel God's presence during this daily meditation, if at all?

Gratitude. Offer thanks to God for giving you the breath of life. Give thanks for the ways in which you felt God's presence before, during, and after your meditation.

Growth. What challenged you today? What came easily today?

Hope. What do you hope tomorrow's meditation practice will bring?

Day Thirty-Seven

DEVOTIONAL MEDITATION

FREEDOM STATEMENT
When I worship God, I am reminded of who I am and whose I am.

OPENING
Be still, and know that I am God. | Be still and know. | Be still. | Be.

PRACTICE
Once you've settled into your breathing pattern, engage in three minutes of devotional meditation. Choose a line from scripture, the Jesus Prayer, a Taizé song, or a hymn or create your own devotional phrase that encapsulates your devotion for and adoration of God. Repeat it to yourself, "gazing" at God in your mind's eye.

CLOSING
Be. | Be still. | Be still and know. | Be still, and know that I am God.

DAILY EXAMEN
God with Us. How did you feel God's presence during this daily meditation, if at all?

Gratitude. Offer thanks to God for giving you the breath of life. Give thanks for the ways in which you felt God's presence before, during, and after your meditation.

Growth. What challenged you today? What came easily today?

Hope. What do you hope tomorrow's meditation practice will bring?

DEVOTIONAL MEDITATION

FREEDOM STATEMENT

Showing devotion to God is as important a spiritual practice as any other. Yet I find it challenging to make time for this and other practices. May I release all that prevents me from drawer nearer to and praising my Source.

OPENING

Be still, and know that I am God. | Be still and know. | Be still. | Be.

PRACTICE

Once you've settled into your breathing pattern, engage in three minutes of devotional meditation. Choose a line from scripture, the Jesus Prayer, a Taizé song, or a hymn or create your own devotional phrase that encapsulates your devotion for and adoration of God. Repeat it to yourself, "gazing" at God in your mind's eye.

CLOSING

Be. | Be still. | Be still and know. | Be still, and know that I am God.

DAILY EXAMEN

God with Us. How did you feel God's presence during this daily meditation, if at all?

Gratitude. Offer thanks to God for giving you the breath of life. Give thanks for the ways in which you felt God's presence before, during, and after your meditation.

Growth. What challenged you today? What came easily today?

Hope. What do you hope tomorrow's meditation practice will bring?

DEVOTIONAL MEDITATION

FREEDOM STATEMENT
Scripture teaches me that I should love the Lord my God with all my heart, mind, body, soul, and strength. May I strive to do my best each day, releasing judgment when I fall short of this command.

OPENING
Be still, and know that I am God. | Be still and know. | Be still. | Be.

PRACTICE
Once you've settled into your breathing pattern, engage in three minutes of devotional meditation. Choose a line from scripture, the Jesus Prayer, a Taizé song, or a hymn or create your own devotional phrase that encapsulates your devotion for and adoration of God. Repeat it to yourself, "gazing" at God in your mind's eye.

CLOSING
Be. | Be still. | Be still and know. | Be still, and know that I am God.

DAILY EXAMEN
God with Us. How did you feel God's presence during this daily meditation, if at all?

Gratitude. Offer thanks to God for giving you the breath of life. Give thanks for the ways in which you felt God's presence before, during, and after your meditation.

Growth. What challenged you today? What came easily today?

Hope. What do you hope tomorrow's meditation practice will bring?

Day Forty

DEVOTIONAL MEDITATION

FREEDOM STATEMENT

Showing devotion to God puts God in God's rightful place in my heart and life. May I continue to free myself to gaze in awe at God. May this attentiveness remain with me.

OPENING

Be still, and know that I am God. | Be still and know. | Be still. | Be.

PRACTICE

Once you've settled into your breathing pattern, engage in three minutes of devotional meditation. Choose a line from scripture, the Jesus Prayer, a Taizé song, or a hymn or create your own devotional phrase that encapsulates your devotion for and adoration of God. Repeat it to yourself, "gazing" at God in your mind's eye.

CLOSING

Be. | Be still. | Be still and know. | Be still, and know that I am God.

DAILY EXAMEN

God with Us. How did you feel God's presence during this daily meditation, if at all?

Gratitude. Offer thanks to God for giving you the breath of life. Give thanks for the ways in which you felt God's presence before, during, and after your meditation.

Growth. What challenged you today? What came easily today?

Hope. What do you hope tomorrow's meditation practice will bring?

Congratulations! You have journeyed through five Christian meditation methods and forty days of meditation. I invite you to return to the beginning of chapter five and complete the forty days again, meditating for an increased amount of time per day (instead of three minutes, try five, seven, or ten) this round. Additionally, return to your daily Examen writings and determine which methods you struggled with and which energized you. Perhaps you'd like to continue your practice with just one or two of the techniques. In chapter seven, you'll have the opportunity to explore exactly how you'd like to proceed with your ongoing meditation practice.

God, you have walked with me through these forty days of Christian meditation. May I continue, one breath at a time, to draw near to you, releasing all judgment and acknowledging that the spiritual life is a practice—not an exercise in perfection. Amen.

Chapter Six

THE SKEPTIC'S JOURNEY— WHAT I LEARNED

"The kingdom of God is not coming with things that can be observed; nor will they say, 'Look, here it is!' or 'There it is!' For, in fact, the kingdom of God is among you."
—Luke 17:20-21

For one who has conquered the mind, the mind is the best of friends, but for one who has not conquered the mind, it acts like one's enemy.

—*The Bhagavad Gita, 6:6*

After twelve months of countless grief counseling sessions and a committed daily meditation practice, I woke up in a panic at 2:00 a.m. on August 8. The day was the first in many milestones marking my mother's hospitalization, hospice care, and ultimate death on August 24. I wasn't experiencing the trauma nightmares with which I'd struggled previously. My dreams weren't filled with scenes of my mother needing a blanket, pain medication, or advocacy. Those dreams dissipated a few months into my meditation practice, just as my therapist had said they would. Following my failed attempt at meditation with Mr. Villain Narrator, I had designed my own curriculum, one in which there were no apps, no tricks, and no shortcuts. I began following it, and the more I breathed deeply, repeated a sacred word, read scripture, extended kindness to myself and to others, and focused on devotion to God during my waking hours, the more peace I felt. Even so, pure anxiety awakened me that particular morning, accompanied by a quickened pulse, elevated blood pressure, and hyper-alertness. My brain had triggered my body's sympathetic nervous system in some way—perhaps unconsciously—telling it to prepare for fight-or-flight for the next sixteen days leading up to the first anniversary of my mother's death.

Immediately, my mind went into overdrive. *Oh, fabulous,* I thought, *now I'm never going to get back to sleep. I'll be exhausted and unproductive all day. I have so much to do; I can't be worrying about this in the middle of the night!* As I continued to contemplate how tired I would be in the morning, the muscle memory of my meditation practice kicked in. I rolled over to my back and placed my hands palms-down on either side of me. I took six deep breaths. *Six deep breaths, Dana. Six deep breaths. Inhale, exhale. Inhale, exhale. You are breathing in the peace of the Holy Comforter. You are lowering your blood pressure with these six deep breaths. Your heart rate will slow. You can stop this autonomic response.* Peace, *your word from the Spirit is* peace. *Peace, peace, peace.*

I don't know how many cycles of breath and centering meditation I practiced in those early morning minutes because I fell asleep soon thereafter. The next morning, it was *still* August 8. My grief remained raw and real, but I was no longer skeptical that I could handle it. I realized then why people meditated consistently—so that they could equip themselves with spiritual coping tools rooted in God and remember the practice during times of stress. That morning, I shuffled to the coffeepot in the way I usually do, tired but not frantic or exhausted, with the 2:00 a.m. wake-up call merely a distant memory. I sat atop the gray *zafu* I'd sat on nearly a year ago. It was broken-in now, with imprints of my (and the cat's) rear end reminding me of my daily commitment. With my phone tucked away in the next room, I had no villainous narrator whispering in my ears. It was just me, using what I had learned to listen to God and experience God's peace. I was no longer a meditation skeptic; I was a meditation practitioner. What I had been practicing every day on the cushion not only shaped me spiritually and allowed me space to hear God but also made God feel close and more readily accessible in times of duress.

Under Construction

My meditation practice didn't come so naturally in the beginning. I dealt with speed bumps, roadblocks, detours, and endless construction. I offered myself grace on the days I felt skeptical or skipped my practice. I was gentle with myself during the weeks in which I simply felt frustrated and distracted. Still, I continued down the road, puttering along like a rusted '92 Geo Prizm. I reminded myself that this was *my* practice and that it was valuable, authentic, and important no matter how many sleek, new Cadillacs passed me along the way.

Over time, the rhythm of the freedom statement, opening ritual, meditation practice, closing ritual, and Examen became second nature. On the second or third round of the forty days, I began practicing all five methods in one sitting. I still didn't practice for long—usually five to ten minutes maximum—but I could transition from breath meditation to centering meditation smoothly, then to *lectio divina*, loving-kindness, and, finally, devotional meditation. The freedom statement prevented me from seeing each session as black and white, all or nothing. The opening and closing rituals called me into and held a meditative space and then released me back into the world. Focusing on my breath helped me stay still and silent. Centering meditation opened me up to God's message for me through the Spirit. *Lectio divina* helped me discern God's will through God's Word. I found that the *lectio divina* passage was usually exactly what I needed for the day, drawing me into God's living Word for my life. Loving-kindness reminded me that I am beloved by God, that others are too, and that I am commanded to love both those who are dear to me and those who are not. I never ran out of enemies to hold in the light, but they became more ridiculous and less personal. Devotional meditation made me realize how selfish I can be in my spiritual life ("God give me this and that, *now!*") and how reluctant I am to focus my attention on devotion toward God. The devotional meditation ended my practice, usually with the Jesus Prayer, because its rhythm coincided with each inhale and exhale.

My time of practicing the Examen each day was invaluable. I recorded what happened—what went well and where I needed growth. Without this time of reflection and writing, I may have given up because I experienced so many days when I felt as if I wasn't making progress. But the Examen kept me focused on hope and gratitude. Without gratitude, the weeds of bitterness and resentment can choke the gardens of our hearts where we plant God's seeds of love and joy.

A year of meditation uncovered struggles. Who knew breathing *on purpose* is far harder than breathing without realizing it? Centering meditation yielded curious words. That first week, I landed on *starve*—perhaps from the Spirit, perhaps not. It didn't make sense at the time. *Is God telling me I'm hungry?* I wondered. Later, I realized God was indeed sending me that message. I was *starving* for connection, *theoria*, that intense "gazing" in which my attention is focused on God and not me. *Lectio divina* had its prickly days, like the reminder from Isaiah 55:8: "My thoughts are not your thoughts, nor are your ways my ways." Ouch. This was a recurring theme throughout my meditation journey: *This is not about pushing your agenda, Dana, the way your prayers have always been. This is about listening for God's voice and experiencing God's presence amid grief and joy.* Loving-kindness cut straight to the heart of improving my own self-talk and judgment of others. And I found, despite some grimacing, a softening toward those for whom I felt anger. Devotional meditation, though clunky at first, became as natural as any worship service I had attended. It provided a time of praise and worship for my heart and mind. This meditation method was the culmination of my journey, reminding me that thinking about, reflecting on, gazing at, and contemplating God makes me spiritually open to God's movement in and through me.

I learned these lessons over time, not overnight. My forty days of meditation, repeated over and over, showed me where God's presence was stirring in my life and my soul, even when I didn't realize it. Eventually, I looked forward to my meditation time—even if it was only five minutes. Instead of rushing through my practice, I relished it. I learned to savor those minutes of quiet surrender to what God was telling me. But every day wasn't coming up roses. The garden of spiritual practice blooms over time, and I felt thorns along the way.

Perfect Is the Enemy of Good

Every two years, the ecumenical Festival of Faith & Writing convenes at Calvin College in Grand Rapids, Michigan. It's a writer's dream retreat, overflowing with inspiring keynotes, pragmatic panels and workshops, and endless networking. The Festival of Faith & Writing is the only conference I've ever attended that is simultaneously invigorating and depleting at a mental and emotional level. It's three days of nonstop inspiration and creativity and, in equal measure, doubt and insecurity. Forging a successful writing career amid a backdrop of literary giants is just a wee bit intimidating and potentially discouraging. The first year I attended, fellow author Whitney R. Simpson, a certified yoga instructor and spiritual director, and I offered five sessions on Christian meditation, using the methods outlined in chapter five.

Whitney and I led our fellow conference-goers through morning and afternoon meditation in a wood-floored art gallery where long streams of fabric and paper leaves hung from skylights. Our sessions were popular; they attracted deer-in-the-headlights writers like ourselves, overstimulated by the buzzing industry of Christian publishing. On day two, after I taught my first session, feelings of inadequacy overwhelmed me. I escaped the art gallery quickly to stand in a far-too-long coffee line, where I stared into my phone, managing to look preoccupied so no one would talk to me. Desperate for caffeine and affirmation, I texted Fred, swallowing my tears before they could expose me. Then my editor—who is one of my best friends—called my name: "Dana."

I was pulled from texting to the present. Joanna was meeting at a table with another Upper Room Books author and asked me to join them after I retrieved my drink. I obliged, but Joanna sensed something was off. The three of us sat for a brief chat, and then Joanna and I were alone. I told her I was doubting my Christian meditation project and needed help—something Enneagram Type 2 (Helpers) hate to ask of others. Joanna offered her ear, her heart, and her help. I cried and blubbered on about how I couldn't meditate—and how I surely couldn't teach or write about it.

"I don't know anything about this meditation world," I told her, my fatalistic, all-or-nothing thoughts getting the best of me. "There's so much I haven't learned or read! I don't know what I'm doing." Joanna listened in the encouraging way she always does, as if I were the only person who existed in the world and I had not already made her ten minutes late for a meeting with a prospective author.

"But you're a researcher," she said. "I know you'll keep learning and digging. That's what I love about your books; I always feel smarter after I read them."

Joanna reminded me that making a meditation practice my own doesn't mean making it perfect. We're all beginners; we're all students. In exploring meditation—and in writing this book—I held space for *practice,* not perfection. No one expected me to be a seasoned expert straight out of the gate. I *would* keep learning and digging, even when I was confronted with how much I didn't yet know. Meditation—and the spiritual life—is about *humility.* We are not God; we will never know everything. Keeping a student's posture gives us permission to be curious and aim for growth. Meditation doesn't require me to achieve outrageous milestones immediately; instead, I aim to make a little progress each day, leaning into grace and gratitude along the way. Ultimately, that is enough.

After Whitney and I taught those five meditation sessions at Festival of Faith & Writing, a theme became abundantly clear: We all yearn for space to practice. Much like the early church monastics withdrew to the wilderness because the institutionalized church no longer filled that need, today's Christians feel that same tug. We have become too entrenched in our own noise—our jam-packed worship routines and prayer formulas—that we have drowned out God's voice. We need quiet practices like breath meditation, centering meditation, *lectio divina* meditation, loving-kindness meditation, and devotional meditation to facilitate our listening to and experiencing God.

I've learned that I shouldn't worry about not knowing enough or seeking a perfect practice. These are traps that place me and my ego in the center of spiritual practice, not God. Humility keeps me reliant on God for guidance; curiosity and persistence help me remain in a mind-set focused on growth. My meditation practice allows me to deepen my connection with God and others.

Glenmary Home Missioners Retreat

Shortly after attending the Festival of Faith & Writing, I led a four-day retreat in the Tennessee mountains with twenty Catholics who were priests (ordained to preside over Mass) and brothers (ordained to preside over some sacraments), and coworkers (called to do the lay work of the church). Glenmary Home Missioners is a religious order founded in 1939 by a Catholic father who saw great need in the rural Appalachian area of the United States. Father Bishop (yes, that was his last name) founded Glenmary in hopes that Catholics could provide ministry to both the Catholic minorities in the area and to the general population of the entire region. Like many religious orders, Glenmarians are gracious and modest. They live simply and drive hours every day to serve the poor and marginalized, particularly Spanish-speaking residents who live in constant fear of deportation. The Glenmarians asked this Baptist clergy-woman to lead a retreat on sabbath because they—like all clergy and laypersons—struggle to embrace the biblical commandment to balance their busy lives (and the endless needs of others) with rest, worship, and community.

The Glenmary retreat was unlike any I'd led not only because it was Catholic but also because I showed up as a different teacher. By the time I met the Glenmarians, I'd been meditating with my forty-day curriculum for nearly four months. My meditation practice was still clunky; I was learning to embrace a daily spiritual practice that I'd never consistently kept before. Father Neil, the retreat coordinator, and I decided to anchor the retreat in both the Liturgy of Hours, a schedule of prayers and Mass, and meditation on scripture (*lectio divina*). All twenty participants—including myself—kept the Hours each day. We held morning and evening prayer together, as well as midday Mass with *lectio divina* sprinkled throughout the day. Before didactic sessions and gatherings for reflection and contemplation, I led the participants through meditation.

The priests, brothers, coworkers, and I steeped ourselves in deep spiritual practice for four days. Whether we felt called to it, wanted it, or weren't quite sure what to do with it, we had no shortage of quiet, contemplative time to listen for God's voice. Through the Liturgy of Hours, *lectio divina*, centering meditation, and devotional meditation, we encountered God in the silence. Normally, such a strict daily regimen of prayer and silence would make me want to run away. But the Glenmarians welcomed the added meditation opportunities and graciously invited me into their own daily rhythm of faithful Catholic practice.

By the second full day of keeping the Hours and three daily meditation sessions of *lectio divina*, I found myself in unfamiliar space: I no longer felt concerned with the outside world. I normally base my identity on what's going on *outside* myself, often tying my worth to how useful or helpful I am to others. Typically, when I'm isolated or quiet, my mind goes into overdrive: *I need to do something for someone, encourage someone, affirm someone, be needed. Who am I if I'm not constantly serving others?* Instead, at this retreat, my mind was unusually calm. I looked forward to refilling my well and receiving—not necessarily helping—during corporate meditation and liturgical times. Gone was my obsession with being effective, needed, known, seen, and credited for helping. The symptoms that usually surface in my effort to be noticed and appreciated—crafting clever tweets, snapping Instagrammable selfies, and posting heartfelt Facebook updates—dissipated. Within those two days of cloistered, contemplative practice with the Glenmarians, I could *hear* and *feel* God's presence—and the chaos of my ego-absorbed, helper mentality diminished. Meditation in community taught me the beauty of *receiving*.

Light as a Feather

The wonder of practicing anything over time is that we make loads of mistakes. Along the way, those missteps can lead us to discover "hacks," ways to make habits more accessible and appealing. So often, I'm guilty of thinking that a routine—spiritual or otherwise—cannot be adapted. Meditation is about connecting, reconnecting, and turning our focus back to God, but we must make it work for *us*. Here are a few hacks I learned that may be useful for you too.

Breath Meditation

If focusing on your breathing in the silence proves difficult, try the following: Place your hands on your stomach to remind yourself to take deep "belly breaths." Repeat to yourself *inhale, exhale.* Alternatively, count: *Inhale, 2, 3, 4; exhale, 3, 2, 1.* The counting slows me down and helps me focus on breathing smoothly and deeply. I also love to picture a feather (like the one on the cover of this book) in front of my face as I inhale and exhale. When I inhale, the feather drops to my mouth; as I exhale, it pushes upward toward my forehead. This visualization helps me find my breathing rhythm on days when it's not coming naturally.

Centering Meditation

Don't be surprised if your centering word is derived from that day's freedom statement. The freedom statement is designed both to release you from judgment and to help set and keep your daily intention. Perhaps something from that day's statement is what the Spirit wants and needs you to sit with. Be open to that. When and if an obscure word emerges (like *starve* for me), be gentle with yourself. Don't overanalyze. You may need a few hours or days to understand what God is stirring within you.

Lectio Divina *Meditation*

This practice helped me fall in love with scripture again because I could use my beginner's mind instead of my exegetical, analytical brain. Scripture is complex, and often we become so bogged down with its meaning that we neglect its mystery. I kept all the verses short in this book, allowing for intense concentration on a particular phrase or image. I learned that less is more; I felt more creativity and less overwhelm with shorter passages. Alternatively, you may want to read other devotional material in addition to or instead of scripture to practice *lectio divina.* I suggest the short meditations found in *The Upper Room* daily devotional guide (www. upperroom.org).

Loving-Kindness Meditation

A lot of baggage emerged with this practice. I had more unresolved tension in certain relationships than I realized—and God never failed to reveal it. When I struggled with sending others God's love and light, I imagined that I'd just swallowed a miniature orb of God's glowing, warm sunlight. Then, the light was *in me* and glowing from me, such that I could freely extend it to others—just as Jesus commands us to do in John 15:12: "Love one another as I have loved you."

Devotional Meditation

This always felt like all five meditation methods rolled into one, which is why I made it the last technique in this book. I found that my practice was most effective if I chose a devotional statement that corresponded with my breathing rhythm. If I could break the statement between an inhale and exhale, then I could concentrate on God more easily throughout the repetition.

Sacred Flaws Lead to Sacred Gems

One week after the first anniversary of my mother's death and nearly a year after I began my meditation practice, I attended a two-hour meditation workshop led by a Hindu couple—one a licensed clinical social worker and both teachers and practitioners of over forty years.[1] I was the only Christian in the room and felt nervous at the prospect of discussing meditation among thirty or so seasoned religious folks whose ancient tradition not only preceded Christianity but also held contemplative practice as a keystone of its faith and tradition. Though I'd practiced my own curriculum and seen improvements in my meditation abilities, I felt humbled to sit among these practitioners. I was exactly what Thomas Merton said I'd be: a beginner.

As the first hour unfolded and I listened dutifully, I was surprised. I might as well have been attending a Christian Sunday school class or a church small group because the spiritual struggles and obstacles expressed by the attendees were just as familiar. I had imagined Hindus, with their several-thousand-year history of meditation, would have nailed this practice. But so many confessed their vulnerabilities and difficulties. They too encountered roadblocks while trying to strengthen their bonds with God. They spoke of meditation as the "umbilical cord" to God—the tie that nurtures them, provides stress relief, and allows them to live into a higher, spiritual purpose. But the Hindus—much like many Christians—confessed that time, children, responsibilities, interest, prioritization, apathy, and faith were all obstacles that kept them from a keeping a consistent meditation practice.[2]

The teachers asked, "How do you feel on a 'good' meditation day? How do you feel on a 'bad' or 'no' meditation day?" Practitioners replied that when they made time in the morning for "good" meditation (which, to me, means *any* amount of time focused on God), God provided dividends on that time, stretching out into a day that held more meaning and less frantic running about. On a "good" meditation day, they felt as if they were standing on "level ground," that they could "be love," that "God had made an altar in their heart," and that they could be "responsive instead of reactive" to stress and anxiety that arose during the day. What happened on a "bad" or "no" meditation day? One Hindu summed it up best: His mind was "Gone with the wind!"[3] Everyone laughed knowingly, including myself.

Then, the teachers asked us the following question: "If history and experience teach you that meditation improves your daily life on many levels and you can name the obstacles that prevent you from practicing, then how can you motivate yourself to continue your meditation practice?" The teachers encouraged us to rank our feelings, zero (not at all or none) to ten (much), in five categories: desire, effort, priority, faith, and taste. Desire: How badly do you want to meditate? Effort: How much energy do you put into your practice? Priority: How much of a priority is your meditation practice? Faith: How much faith do you have that meditation makes a difference in your daily life? Taste: How much do you hunger for, yearn for, and ultimately enjoy your connection with God?[4]

The Hindu teachers emphasized that a healthy meditation practice includes a consistent examination of the effects of our "good," "bad," and/or "no" meditation days, as well as our motivations behind the practice. But they also offered grace. We needn't degrade ourselves when our practice doesn't go as expected. Instead, we can remember that the mind—which we are harnessing to focus its attention on God—is like a toddler or teenager: stubborn, restless, tantrum-prone, irritable, and uncooperative. Therefore, we must nurture our minds as we would children, giving them love, limits, and consistency.[5]

To give the mind love, limits, and consistency, we need to practice. Meditating poorly for one or three minutes is better than not meditating at all. Even a hint of meditation keeps the channel to God open. The teachers urged us to bring a good intention to our practice; we can't enter our meditation space with low expectations, believing that our practice will be boring or a waste of time. Instead, we can encourage ourselves to pay attention, remembering that even a few minutes focused on God can be holy and energizing. Lastly, the teachers reminded us that gratitude is essential. Having the privilege of reading about, learning about, and taking time to practice meditation is a sacred luxury for which we should give God thanks. Doing so, in turn, increases the joy of our practice.[6]

A Way of Life

There was no shortage of lessons learned this year—from beginning my practice after my mother's death to practicing at the Hindu meditation workshop and all the stepping stones in between. My Examen journal is full of the realizations, joys, and struggles I encountered along the way. I included gratitude for the days that I practiced even when I felt like it wasn't working or wasn't worth the time. I believe most of us don't stick with spiritual practices because we believe we must get them right or they don't "count." So often, we fail to see that God's not keeping score and that the time we spend meeting God—whatever that looks like—is well spent. No matter when or why we begin our meditation practice—in times of grief, after a health crisis, because of advice from a friend (or therapist), or as a way to combat anxiety, stress, and loneliness, meditation offers us the opportunity to rediscover ourselves and God.

Meditation practice is not another to-do to add to our daily lists but a way of life. It shapes our faith journey and cultivates and deepens our relationship with God, which, in turn, affects our relationships with one another—and all of creation. When we begin with *listening* and *experiencing* God each day, we realign ourselves with God's still small voice. This new way of life doesn't require a total upheaval, remodel, or demolition. It simply starts with a beginner's mind and a longing to connect with God, one breath at a time.

Chapter Seven

THE READER'S JOURNEY—
WHAT YOU LEARNED

If the doors of my heart ever close, I am as good as dead.

—Mary Oliver

Contemplation is also the response to a call: a call from [God] Who has no voice, and yet Who speaks in everything that is, and Who, most of all, speaks in the depths of our own being: for we ourselves are words of [God's].

—Thomas Merton

Our lives are shaped by long days, short years, frustrating people, inconveniences, and a chaotic world in need of love and healing. We are not static. We are dynamic, shaped and molded by each moment and experience. The spiritual life is about opening the doors of our soul and taking a look inside. At their essence, all contemplative spiritual practices crack open our hardened, restless hearts, weary and worn from life. Spiritual practices soften us, slow us, and allow God's light and voice to enter us, so that we can, in turn, shine that light and love toward others. But it's hard to slow down. It's hard to breathe. It's hard to meditate—or even to say we're going to meditate. It's hard to maintain a spiritual practice of any kind, especially one that urges us to be still and examine our heart, mind, and soul.

Beginning and maintaining a meditation practice doesn't mean that we must escape to a mountain cave and remain silent the rest of our lives to reconnect with God. That's not sustainable—and it's certainly not realistic or accessible. Instead, we can keep an authentic practice right here and right now, even amid chaos, endless distractions, and our need for perfection. The world isn't going anywhere; what matters, though, is how we engage (or don't) with it.

Meditation in the Real World

About six months after I began my own forty-day practice, I taught some of these meditation methods to the eager members of my beloved Binkley Baptist Church in Chapel Hill, North Carolina. I've attended Binkley for twenty years, learning alongside pilgrims in search of the truest way of living and being the gospel.

They say that you teach what you most need to learn, and so it was that at a Wednesday night supper of vegetarian soup and Caesar salad made by my favorite local chefs who are also Binkley members, I learned an important meditation lesson. Meditating in church with other people is not like communal, extemporaneous prayer, which comes naturally for many Christians, especially Baptists. Group meditation and silence can be awkward and downright funny. As both the leader and a participant, I couldn't help but notice the people around me: *Is that man sleeping?* I wondered. *What's on her mind?* Bellies full, we propelled forward in this one-hour Lenten session on meditation. With only one full week of Lent remaining, I encouraged the twenty-five participants to use those last days of the wilderness season to practice breath meditation, loving-kindness meditation, and devotional meditation.

As I walked the participants through each of the methods and into brief, three-minute sessions, the most important lesson of spiritual practice emerged for us all. During breath meditation, someone outside the room where we were gathered *slowly* and *deliberately* slid a large, heavy metal table down the length of the 100-foot linoleum hallway. During the loving-kindness meditation, cell phones furiously vibrated in the participants' bags, as if every aunt, best friend, or telemarketer needed to get in touch with them at the same time. Then, during the devotional meditation, as if on cue, a loud gang of playful children danced down the hall, shouting and singing. Over and over, the lessons arrived: Meditation doesn't happen in a noiseless vacuum. We practice in the real world, with sounds and interruptions and distractions and minds that cannot help themselves from darting around. Our scriptural and theological calling is to do it anyway—amid the noise and chaos—just as Jesus did.

Your Map to the Interior

Each semester, I teach two sections of a critical thinking course to Wake Technical Community College students. In that course, I equip students with tools that train them *how* to think instead of telling them *what* to think. In their evaluation of arguments, they learn how to spot fallacies—flaws in reasoning. They quickly realize that fallacies are all around us—and that most of us have committed nearly *every single one*. Americans, in particular, practice a certain flaw in reasoning that is especially harmful to us and to others. We fall into the trap of thinking that we can be perfect at everything—usually overnight and without much effort.

And though this thinking is incorrect for just about any skill, it certainly isn't how we should approach meditation.

Meditation is about *practice*. We do not master God; we do not master our relationships with one another. Instead, we lean into growth that comes from stepping into a dynamic practice that is shaped day after day. Our meditation practice will never be perfect—nor should it be. We've even seen evidence of this imperfection in testimonies from monastics, saints, and mystics. These ordinary humans—like us—devoted their entire lives (or much of their lives) to connecting with and serving God and neighbor, but they did not view themselves as having "mastered" contemplation. That is not the human experience. Instead, when we read the personal writings of Julian of Norwich, Teresa of Ávila, Saint Teresa of Calcutta, Thomas Merton, or Dr. Martin Luther King Jr., we resonate with their spiritual journeys because they've shared both the incredible moments of sensing the sacred and the ordinary moments of doubt. Both play integral roles in the spiritual life.

Your Turn

Now that you have equipped yourself with the scriptural, theological, and scientific aspects of meditation and you've dipped your toes into forty days of practice, where would you like to go? Return to the questions in chapter one and review your responses. What intention did you set for your journey? What happened? What would you like to tweak or change moving forward? What does this continued path look like for you as an individual, as a small group, or as a parish?

What follows are exploratory questions designed for you to visualize how your practice might continue to unfold. Many of these questions have been adapted from the meditation workshop I attended.[1]

When/how did you feel God's presence as you moved through the forty days of practice?

How did you feel on a "good" meditation day?

How did you feel on a "bad" or "no" meditation day?

What fruit has your forty-day meditation practice already grown?

What do you long for from your continued meditation practice? What fruit do you hope it will bear in the future?

Of the five, what meditation method energized you most? What meditation method challenged you most?

Rate each of these categories based on your first forty days of practice (zero is none/not at all, ten is a lot, five is average/somewhat): Desire (How badly do you want to meditate?); Effort (How much energy do you put into your meditation practice?); Priority (How much of a priority is your meditation practice?); Faith (How much faith do you have that meditation will make a difference in your daily life?); Taste (How much do you hunger for, yearn for, and ultimately enjoy your connection with God?)

Envision your ideal daily meditation practice. What does your meditation practice look like each day? Be specific. Are you practicing in the morning, midday, or evening? How many minutes per day feels doable? How do you anticipate you will work through setbacks and frustrations?

Being Mindful of the Seasons of Life

Sometimes you may struggle to even sit on the cushion—let alone meditate—and other times your meditation practice comes easily. Try to see both experiences as equal and withhold judgment. What's most important is that you continue to hold the space for silence and listening for God.

Whether it's grief or something else, I know well the difficulty—and often the necessity—of taking on a spiritual practice during tough times. If you feel like me—that rusted-out '92 Geo Prizm compared to everyone else's Cadillacs—don't sweat it. Stay in your lane. Everyone's path is unique and subject to change—for better or for worse. Most importantly, keep showing up, puttering down the road to meet God wherever you are.

Our Permission Slip

Should you feel stuck, remember that you have been given permission to practice meditation by Jesus himself, who sought out "deserted" places to ground himself in God. Jesus is your biggest cheerleader in this practice. He taught it; he led by example. Jesus embraced an authentic method of centering himself in contemplation, and it was often wordless and embodied. You can practice it too. There is nothing wrong with the prayer formulas you've been given or how you've been praying for decades, but meditation offers you an additional tool—a different way to connect to, listen for, and become aware of God's presence. There is no greater gift than that. Remember the psalmist's words, and place them on a sticky note anywhere you practice: "Be still, and know that I am God!" Jesus knew that to be true too.

If Jesus were sitting next to your *zafu*, then he'd remind you that his faithful servant and student Thomas Merton said it best: You will always be a beginner, even though you don't want to be. Jesus would also tell you that this means you simply must take it from the top, once more, from the beginning—*one breath at a time.*

APPENDIX

Once you've completed the forty-day journey, you may want to return to this page for a reminder of the steps for each meditation method.

Breath Meditation: Focus on your inhale and exhale. Breathe deeply and smoothly. Feel the Spirit of the Living God within you and all around you. Imagine God to be in each breath.

Centering Meditation: As you smooth and deepen your breath, invite the Spirit to offer you a word for the day. Hold that word in your mind's eye and repeat it. Consider its meaning for you that day.

Lectio Divina **Meditation:** Using a daily scripture reading (including the additional readings below and on the following page), look or listen for a word or phrase that "shimmers." What is God inviting you to hear through this word or phrase?

Loving-Kindness Meditation: Extend God's love to yourself, your loved ones, your enemies, and all God's creation through these phrases:

May I/[name] be safe.
May I/[name] be healthy.
May I/[name] be happy.
May I/[name] be at peace.

Devotional Meditation: Use this time to lift your praise and adoration to God. Repeat a line from your favorite hymn, the Jesus Prayer, or other mantra of your own choosing that shows your reverence and awe for God. Use your devotional phrase to fix your attention and focus upon God.

Additional Scripture Passages for *Lectio Divina* Meditation

- Jeremiah 6:16
- Matthew 6:6
- Matthew 6:9

- Matthew 26:39
- Matthew 26:42
- Mark 1:35
- Matthew 5:44-45
- Romans 8:6
- Galatians 5:25
- Philippians 4:4-9
- 1 Thessalonians 5:17

Additional Resources/Books on Contemplative Prayer and Meditation

- À Kempis, Thomas. *The Imitation of Christ.* New York: Dover Publications, 1940.
- De Mello, Anthony. *Sadhana, a Way to God: Christian Exercises in Eastern Form.* New York: Image Books, 1978.
- Foster, Richard J. and James Bryan Smith, eds. *Devotional Classics: Selected Readings for Individuals and Groups, Rev. Ed.* San Francisco: HarperOne, 2005.
- McGinn, Bernard, ed. *The Essential Writings of Christian Mysticism.* New York: Random House, 2006.
- Merton, Thomas. *Contemplative Prayer.* New York: Image Books, 1969.
- Palmer, G. E. H, Philip Sherrard, and Kallistos Ware. *The Philokalia: The Complete Text, Volume II,* compiled by St. Nikodimos of the Holy Mountain and St. Makarios of Corinth. New York: Farrar, Straus and Giroux, 1983.
- Willard, Dallas. *The Spirit of the Disciplines: Understanding How God Changes Lives.* New York: HarperCollins, 1988.

NOTES

Chapter Two: The Case for Meditation

1. Henrik Rydell Johnsén, "The Early Jesus Prayer and Meditation in Greco-Roman Philosophy," *Meditation in Judaism, Christianity and Islam: Cultural Histories* (New York: Bloomsbury Academic, 2013), 1, 3–4.
2. *JPS Tanakh Customer Guide,* The Jewish Publication Society, jps.org.
3. "Hagah," *Strong's Hebrew Concordance*, #1897, BibleHub.com.
4. "Meletao," *Strong's Greek Dictionary of the New Testament*, #3191, Lexiconcordance.com.
5. Tellihum (Psalms) 1: Septuagint, *Blue Letter Bible*, BlueLetterBible.org.
6. Jeffrey Brodd et al. *Invitations to World Religions*, 2nd ed. (New York: Oxford University Press, 2016), 366.
7. *Psalmi I, Chapter 1,* Vulgate.org.
8. Maria Carrico, "Get to Know the Eight Limbs of Yoga," *Yoga Journal* (August 28, 2007): 3. www.yoga-journal.com/practice/the-eight-limbs.
9. Carrico.
10. Carrico, 3.
11. "Theoria," *Strong's Greek Concordance*, #2335, BibleHub.com.
12. John R. Tyson, ed., *Invitation to Christian Spirituality: An Ecumenical Anthology* (New York: Oxford University Press, 1999), 33.
13. Tyson, 33.
14. Tyson, 34.
15. Tyson, 34.
16. Tyson, 34.
17. Tyson., 34.
18. Tyson, 49.
19. Tyson, 49.

Chapter Three: The Power of Breath

1. Nicholas Carr, "How Smartphones Hijack Our Brains," *The Wall Street Journal,* October 7, 2017, ProQuest Central.
2. Aaron Smith, "Record shares of Americans now own smartphones, have home broadband," Pew Research Center, January 17, 2017, http://www.pewresearch.org/fact-tank/2017/01/12/evolution-of-technology/.
3. Carr, "How Smartphones Hijack Our Brains."
4. Michaeleen Doucleff and Allison Aubrey, "Smartphone Detox: How to Power Down in a Wired World," *NPR*, February 12, 2018, https://www.npr.org/sections/health-shots/2018/02/12/584389201/smartphone-detox-how-to-power-down-in-a-wired-world.
5. Doucleff and Aubrey.

6. Gregory Bassham et al., *Critical Thinking: A Student's Introduction*, 5th ed. (New York: McGraw-Hill, 2013), 322.

7. Ron Joines, MD, MPH, in discussion with author, July and August 2018.

8. Joines.

9. Joines.

10. Marc A. Russo, Danielle M. Santarelli, and Dean O'Rourke, "The Physiological Effects of Slow Breathing in the Healthy Human," *Breathe* (2017), 13: 298–309, 299.

11. Russo, Santarelli, and O'Rourke, 300–1.

12. Russo, Santarelli, and O'Rourke, 303.

13. Russo, Santarelli, and O'Rourke, 303.

14. Russo, Santarelli, and O'Rourke, 304.

15. Russo, Santarelli, and O'Rourke, 304–5.

16. Russo, Santarelli, and O'Rourke, 305.

17. Russo, Santarelli, and O'Rourke, 305.

18. Mark B. Detweiler et al., "Treatment of Post-Traumatic Stress Disorder Nightmares at a Veterans Affairs Medical Center," *Journal of Clinical Medicine* 5, no. 12 (December 2016): 2, MDPI.

19. Hisao Mori et al., "How Does Deep Breathing Affect Office Blood Pressure and Pulse Rate?" *Hypertension Research* 28, no. 6 (2005): 499–504.

20. Mori et al., 499–504.

Chapter Four: The How of Meditation

1. Whitney R. Simpson, *Holy Listening with Breath, Body, and the Spirit* (Nashville, TN: Upper Room Books, 2016), 21.

2. Sharon Seyfarth Garner, *Mandalas, Candles, and Prayer: A Simply Centered Advent* (Nashville, TN: Upper Room Books, 2017), 25–26.

Chapter Five: Practice, Not Perfection

1. Garner, *Mandalas, Candles, and Prayer*, 96–99.

2. Simpson, *Holy Listening*, 23.

3. Garner, *Mandalas, Candles, and Prayer*, 73–74.

4. Simpson, *Holy Listening*, 23–24.

5. Bob Stahl and Elisha Goldstein, *A Mindfulness-Based Stress Reduction Workbook* (Oakland, CA: New Harbinger Publications, Inc., 2010), 135–36.

Chapter Six: The Skeptic's Journey—What I Learned

1. Arcana Sidi and Karnamrita Das, "Japa Meditation Workshop," September 1, 2018, Mill Spring, NC.

2. Sidi and Das.

3. Sidi and Das.

4. Sidi and Das.

5. Sidi and Das.

6. Sidi and Das.

Chapter Seven: The Reader's Journey—What You Learned

1. Arcana Sidi and Karnamrita Das, "Japa Meditation Workshop," September 1, 2018, Mill Spring, NC.